INDONESIA MATTERS

INDONESIA MATTERS
Asia's Emerging Democratic Power

Amitav Acharya
American University, USA

World Scientific

NEW JERSEY · LONDON · SINGAPORE · BEIJING · SHANGHAI · HONG KONG · TAIPEI · CHENNAI

Published by

World Scientific Publishing Co. Pte. Ltd.

5 Toh Tuck Link, Singapore 596224

USA office: 27 Warren Street, Suite 401-402, Hackensack, NJ 07601

UK office: 57 Shelton Street, Covent Garden, London WC2H 9HE

National Library Board, Singapore Cataloguing-in-Publication Data
Acharya, Amitav, author.
    Indonesia matters : Asia's emerging democratic power / Amitav Acharya.--Singapore :
World Scientific Publishing Co. Pte. Ltd., [2014]
    pages cm
    ISBN 978-981-46-3206-5 (hardcover)
    ISBN 978-981-46-1985-1 (paperback)
    1. Indonesia--Foreign relations. 2. Indonesia--Politics and government--1998–   I. Title.
    DS638
    327.598--dc23

OCN883177669

British Library Cataloguing-in-Publication Data
A catalogue record for this book is available from the British Library.

Typeset by Stallion Press
Email: enquiries@stallionpress.com

CONTENTS

Preface

vii

Abbreviations

xi

Chapter 1

Why Indonesia Matters?

1

Chapter 2

Democracy, Development and Stability:

Creating a Virtuous Cycle

19

Chapter 3

Indonesia and the Regional Architecture

49

Chapter 4

Indonesia and the Major Powers

75

Chapter 5
Indonesia as a Global Actor
99

Chapter 6
A Nation on the Move: Indonesian Voices
119

About the Author
135

PREFACE

T his book grew primarily out of a series of conversations I have had with Indonesians about their country's foreign policy and role in regional and international affairs. I have always been fascinated by a country which, despite not being the number one military or economic power in its own region, has been able to provide leadership and direction not only to Southeast Asia, but also to the wider Asia-Pacific region. And it is emerging as a recognized and respected voice in world affairs.

This is not a book about Indonesia's domestic politics, nor is it a comprehensive account of Indonesia's foreign policy in general. Rather it offers a snapshot of Indonesia's role as an emerging power in Asia and in the world. I will discuss what I mean by "emerging power" in Chapter 1, but suffice is to say that it focuses on those aspects of Indonesia's role which have wider regional and global relevance and implications. While the country's bilateral relations are factored in, I give more focus to regional and multilateral relationships as would be consistent with the notion of an emerging power.

A good deal of this book focuses on the Presidency of Susilo Bambang Yudhoyono (2004–14). This is an important turning point for Indonesia for three reasons. First, this is the period when Indonesia emerged from its domestic economic and political crisis with a sense of having consolidated its democracy. Yudhoyono became the first directly elected President of Indonesia, the first to be re-elected and the first to complete his two elected terms. Second, and especially important for the theme of this book, it is under the Yudhoyono presidency that Indonesia acquired international recognition as an emerging power. This was the result of its democratic consolidation, economic growth, and relative stability, as well as its robust re-engagement with ASEAN and its place and role in the G-20 (Group of 20), which became a summit-level global forum in 2008. Third, Yudhoyono has been an unusually active foreign policy president, who, even his critics concede, has worked energetically to advance Indonesia's image and influence in the region and in the world.

In his conversations with me, the President took particular care to stress that Indonesia's achievements are not his alone, and that Indonesia still faces major challenges in advancing itself as an emerging power. As befits the leader of a democracy with a free and vibrant media, Yudhoyono is openly criticized and praised within Indonesia. But for many in the international community, he has been *the* symbol of Indonesia's leadership aspirations and role in regional and international affairs with a style that is widely recognized as gentle, open, and engaging. As he steps down from office, only time will tell how much of his legacy will endure. It is possible that Indonesia under a future leader will go from strength to strength or it might become less active and more inward looking in its foreign policy, or its domestic politics might take an authoritarian turn. No matter what happens, Yudhoyono's presidency will be remembered as a period in which a vast and immensely diverse country made significant strides in making a virtuous cycle out of democracy, development and stability into a virtuous cycle and considerably enhanced its international standing and role.

A good deal of foreign commentary on Indonesia's political future, including its prospects as an emerging power, ignores voices from within the country. I have tried to tell the story of Indonesia by drawing on conversations with people *inside* the country, from its President in Jakarta to the head of a *pondok pesantren* (Islamic boarding school) in Sulawesi.

Indonesia is a nation of extraordinarily hospitable people. Over the past two decades, from the Suharto era to the present, I have had the good fortune to visit Indonesia dozens of times, and to talk to numerous experts and officials, including its Foreign Ministers (the late Ali Alatas was extremely generous to me), military commanders, politicians and human rights activists, while conducting research topics such as ASEAN cooperation, human rights and democracy in Southeast Asia, the 1955 Asia-Africa Conference in Bandung, and Indonesia's foreign policy and international role more generally. Every time, I have been deeply touched by the willingness of its intellectuals, officials, media and civil society activists to receive me, provide me with information, offer comments and suggestions and engage me in discussions and debates. For this book,

I can only mention a few of them, since a good deal of my conversations were with people who did not want to be identified or whose identity I did not note down (to encourage candour).

President Susilo Bambang Yudhoyono, President of Indonesia
Marty Natalegawa, Foreign Minister of Indonesia
Hassan Wirajuda, former Foreign Minister
Purnomo Yusgiantoro, Defence Minister, and his staff
Dino Patti Djalal, Ambassador to the US (2010–13)
Budi Bowoleksono, Director-General of the Indonesian Foreign Ministry (who succeeded Djlal as Indonesia's Ambassador to the US)
Mahendra Siregar, Chairman of the Indonesia Investment Coordinating Board and its G-20 "Sherpa"
Sidarto Danusubroto, Speaker of the People's Consultative Assembly (MPR-Majelis Permusyawaratan Rakyat)
Kemal Stamboel, former member of the DPR and former Chairman of the First Commission of the House of Representative of Indonesia (Komisi I Dewan Perwakilan Rakyat-DPR), currently Secretary-General of the Foreign Banks Association of Indonesia (FBAI)
Teuku *Faizasyah*, Spokesman for President Yudhoyono and former spokesman of the Ministry of Foreign Affairs
Meidyatama Suryodiningra, Editor-in-Chief, *The Jakarta Post*
I Ketut Putra Erawan, Executive Director, Institute for Peace and Democracy, Bali (the IPD is the implementing agency of the Bali Democracy Forum)
Major General Bachtiar, Commander of Kodam VII/Wirabuana, Makassar, and his staff.
God bless Vicky Lumentut, Mayor of Manado
Rizal Sukma, Executive Director, Center for Strategic and International Studies (CSIS), Jakarta
Rahimah Abdulrahim, Executive Director, The Habibie Center
Philips Vermonte, Researcher, Center for Strategic and International Studies (CSIS), Jakarta
Riefqi Muna, Researcher, Center for Political Studies, Indonesian Institute of Sciences
Dr. Afifuddin Harisah, Principal, Pondok An-Nahdlah, Makassar

A special note of thanks to Ambassador Dino Patti Djalal, one of the most energetic and far-sighted diplomats in Washington, D.C. whom I have come across, for his strong encouragement and support for this book, especially in helping with my interviews in Indonesia. I am grateful to The Habibie Center, founded by the former President of the Republic of Indonesia, B. J. Habibie and focusing on human rights and democracy, for providing me with valuable briefings and information on the country's domestic conflicts. Benjamin Schreer of the Australian Strategic Policy Institute kindly shared his research on Indonesian defence spending and military acquisitions, as presented in Chapter 4. I thank Adam Tuigo and Sade Bimantara, from the Indonesian Foreign Ministry, for their generous support and advice for this book. This book would not have been completed without the timely and excellent research assistance provided by Wirya Adiwena in Jakarta and Nadia Bulkin, Allan Layug, and Chakra Pratima in Washington, D.C. Chapter 2, especially the sections dealing with Indonesian democracy, development and stability, was first drafted by Bulkin, who had just completed a master's thesis at the American University specializing in Indonesian democracy; she is emerging as one of the most promising young scholars of Indonesian politics and foreign policy.

I thank the World Scientific publishers (Singapore, London and New York), and its Publishing Director Chua Hong Koon for undertaking the publication of this book at very short notice. Last but certainly not the least, I owe a major debt to Triena Ong. As the long-term Managing Editor of the Institute of Southeast Asian Studies in Singapore, she built what is perhaps Southeast Asia's largest and most successful English-language publishing outlet until leaving late last year to join the private sector. Of Indonesian descent, and well versed in the history and current affairs of Indonesia and Southeast Asia, she has provided invaluable assistance with this book, as editor and adviser.

This book was completed — deliberately — before the 9 July 2014 presidential elections, which pitted Joko Widodo against Prabowo Subianto. While I do not discuss the implications of the outcome of that election, the five factors outlined in the conclusion remain relevant in assessing Indonesia's future progress and role as an emerging power under the new president.

ABBREVIATIONS

ABRI	Angkatan Bersenjata Republik Indonesia
ASEAN	Association of Southeast Asian Nations
APEC	Asia-Pacific Economic Cooperation
APC	Armoured Personnel Carriers
ARF	ASEAN Regional Forum
BDF	Bali Democracy Forum
BRICS	Brazil, Russia, India, China, South Africa
CBDR	Common but Differentiated Responsibility
CSIS	Center for Strategic and International Studies (Indonesia)
COC	Code of Conduct (in South China Sea)
DOC	Declaration on Code of Conduct (in South China Sea)
DPD	Dewan Perwakilan Daerah (Regional Representative Council)
DPR	Dewan Perwakilan Rakyat (People's Representative Council)
DPRD	Dewan Perwakilan Rakyat Daerah (DPRD I: Provincial Legislative Council; DPRD II: District Legislative Council)
EAS	East Asia Summit
FPI	Front Pembela Islam (Islamic Defenders' Front)
G-20	Group of 20
GESF	General Expenditure Support Fund (G-20)
IMF	International Monetary Fund
IPD	Institute of Peace and Democracy (Bali)
JI	Jemaah Islamiya
KID	Indonesia Community for Democracy
KPK	Komisi Pemberantasan Korupsi (Corruption Eradication Commission)
KPU	Komisi Pemilihan Umum (General Elections Commission)

LPD	Landing Platform Docks
MDGs	Millennium Development Goals
MEF	Minimum Essential Force
MP3EI	Masterplan Percepatandan Perluasan Pembangunan Ekonomi Indonesia (Masterplan for Acceleration and Expansion of Indonesia's Economic Development
MPR	Majelis Permusyawaratan Rakyat (People's Consultative Assembly)
NAM	Non-Aligned Movement
NATO	North Atlantic Treaty Organization
OBIT	One Billion Indonesian Trees (for the World)
OIC	Organisation of Islamic Cooperation
OICIPHRC	OIC Independent Permanent Human Right Commission
OPEC	Organization of Petroleum Exporting Countries
PKS	Partai Keadilan Sejahtera (Prosperous Justice Party)
PKO	Peace Keeping Operations
PPP	Partai Persatuan Pembangunan (United Development Party)
R2P	Responsibility to Protect
REDD	Reducing Emissions from Deforestation and Forest Degradation
TAC	Treaty of Amity and Cooperation (of ASEAN)
TNI	Tentara Nasional Indonesia (Indonesian National Armed Forces, formerly ABRI)
UN	United Nations
UNCLOS	United Nations Convention on the Law of the Sea
UNORCID	United Nations Office for REDD+ Coordination in Indonesia
UNSC	United Nations Security Council
WTO	World Trade Organization
ZOPFAN	Zone of Peace, Freedom and Neutrality (ASEAN)

Chapter 1

WHY INDONESIA MATTERS?

Indonesia is no longer "a nation in waiting".... Indonesia is a nation whose time has come –
and we are seizing the moment with determination and hard work.

(Indonesian President Susilo Bambang Yudhoyono, May 2011)[1]

If you want to know whether Islam, democracy, modernity and women's rights can co-exist,
go to Indonesia.

(Hillary Clinton, February 2009)[2]

Indonesia is an emerging power of 21st century Asia and world order, but it is not moving towards that position in the traditional manner. The term "emerging powers" recognizes the growing, primarily economic, but also political and strategic, status of a group of nations most, if not all of which were once categorized as (and in some accounts still are) part of the "Third World" or "global South".[3] Indonesia belongs in this category. It is the fourth most populous country in the world after China, India and the United States. It is also the world's largest Muslim majority nation-state and the third largest democracy. Its economy is currently the tenth largest on the global scale, and McKinsey Company predicts that it will become the seventh largest by 2030. Since the fall of the dictatorship of Suharto in 1998, Indonesia has held three direct presidential elections that are free and fair. During the 2000–10 period, its economic growth surpassed all the emerging economies except that of China and India and was ahead of the other BRICS nations Brazil, Russia, and South Africa.

But the Indonesian story suggests a different pathway to emerging power status than that of other nations. This pathway is based not so much on military and/or economic capabilities. Rather, it lies in the ability of a country to develop a positive, virtuous correlation among three factors – democracy, development and stability – while pursuing a foreign policy of restraint towards neighbours

2 • INDONESIA MATTERS

and active engagement with the world at large. This is the key lesson from the story of Indonesia that this book seeks to present.

To elaborate, Indonesia has achieved its newfound prominence in global affairs in a very different manner compared with other emerging powers in the developing world, including the BRICS (Brazil, Russia, India, China and South Africa). Two things set Indonesia apart from most of the other emerging powers. First, while the rise of other BRICS countries focused first and foremost on economic growth and military spending, Indonesia's rise came on the back of democratization and regional engagement. Each member-state of the BRICS is a significant military power – some regionally and some like China and Russia globally. Even the non-BRICS emerging powers such as South Korea, Nigeria and Saudi Arabia had acquired significant regional economic and military clout before their diplomatic and political roles came to be recognized. To further highlight the uniqueness of the Indonesian pathway towards emerging power status, it is sometimes compared with the Scandinavian countries Norway, Sweden and Denmark, or with Australia and Canada, which are called "middle powers".[4] But these countries are wealthy Western nations, and some, such as Sweden and Australia, possess significant military power.

By contrast, Indonesia is still militarily and economically a weak state, especially compared to some of its neighbours. Yet, it enjoys comparable or even greater regional leadership legitimacy and clout than most of the other emerging powers in the developing world. In short, for a country which is neither the strongest military nor the economic power even in its own immediate region (even the tiny Singapore scores more on both counts), Indonesia has done more regional role-playing as a mediator and facilitator in Asian conflicts than the region's major powers, i.e., China, Japan and India.

The second point of difference relates to the position of an emerging power within its own region. The Indonesian story suggests that the key to global status and recognition lies in good regional relations. Foreign Minister Marty Natalegawa describes Indonesia as a "regional power with global interests and concerns".[5] We can modify this description slightly to say that Indonesia pursues a "regionalist path to its global role". According to Natalegawa, many rising powers suffer from a "regional trust deficit" with their neighbours. Indonesia is different. And evidence suggests that there is much truth to it. While relations between powers such as India, China, Japan, South Africa and Brazil with their neighbours are often marked by mistrust and conflict, those of Indonesia are marked by trust and confidence. In fact, Indonesia is universally acknowledged as a regional "elder", and enjoys far more cordial relations with all its neighbours. Thus, a distinctive feature of Indonesia's role as an emerging power is that while it is not even a regionally dominant power in military or economic terms, it is more respected and also expected to play – at minimum – the role of mediator and facilitator in regional crises and conflicts.

"Emerging Power"

In one respect, describing Indonesia as an "emerging" power is anything but new. At the height of its radical anti-colonial foreign policy, President Sukarno divided the world into Old Established Forces (OLDEFOS) and Newly Emerging Forces (NEFOS). He thus juxtaposed the anti-colonial elements in the international system against Western neocolonial hegemony, and placed Indonesia squarely in the front ranks of the emerging forces. But while Indonesia has in the past been regarded as an emerging power, it was not regarded as an emerging *democratic* power. Indeed, Sukarno's dichotomous categories came about after he had instituted a system of "Guided Democracy" for Indonesia in the late 1950s. This system replaced the elected parliament with one in which half of its members were appointed by the President. Today's Indonesia is democratic not only against the standards of Suharto's unabashedly authoritarian New Order, but also against Sukarno's Guided Democracy.

The term "emerging powers" today has no anti-colonial baggage; on the contrary, it refers to countries that have thrived mainly by embracing capitalism.[6] Indeed, it was a Goldman Sachs analyst for emerging markets who contributed to the popularity of the term by coining the word BRIC – Brazil, Russia, India, China – in 2001.[7] The entry of South Africa in 2010 made it into BRICS. But emerging powers is also a term applied to other non-BRICS nations who show a high degree of economic potential and diplomatic dynamism. Indonesia along with Mexico, Argentina, Nigeria, Saudi Arabia, South Korea, and Turkey belongs to this category.

Some analysts make a distinction between "emerging power" and "rising power", associating the latter with countries that have a clear potential to become great powers, such as China, India, and Brazil. "Emerging powers" are not necessarily seen as heading for international great power status. In general, Indonesian leaders do not see their nation as a great power – they are more comfortable viewing it as an emerging power.

Aside from the BRICS, there have been plenty of other "clubs" whose acronyms designate status as emerging markets/powers. Indonesia has been occasionally, but not always, considered to be part of such acronyms. Some are largely notional, such as BRIICS (including Indonesia), BASIC (BRIC minus Russia, but with South Africa), while others are functioning entities, such as IBSA (India, Brazil, South Africa), BRICSAM (add South Africa and Mexico). Other acronyms include CIVETS (Colombia, Indonesia, Vietnam, Egypt, Turkey and South Africa), "breakout nations"[8] (Turkey, Philippines, Thailand, India and Poland, Colombia, South Korea, Nigeria). Still another is MIST (Mexico, Indonesia, South Korea and Turkey). At a broader level, the key point of reference is the G-20,[9] a club known for its importance in global finance, membership in which almost automatically earns a country the label of emerging power.

Some have argued that the BRICS grouping should be extended to include Indonesia. But one does not find too much enthusiasm or expectation among Jakarta's foreign policy circles for this idea. When asked whether Indonesia would like to be part of the BRICS, Hassan Wirajuda, Indonesia's Foreign Minister from 2001 to 2009, told the author: "We don't bother much about it…We have our own game, ASEAN, [and] East Asia." He points out that while Indonesia is not included in the BRICS, "the growth of BRICS has declined, while Indonesia's is growing more rapidly". "What is the meaning of BRICS, or not being included in the BRICS?" he asks. Reminding that Indonesia is projected to be the seventh largest economy in the world by 2030 according to a report by the global consulting firm McKinsey, he believes that "it is more important to be part of East Asia – the centre of gravity of the world, the region of the 21st century".[10]

In the meantime, Indonesia has been included into the "fragile five" which includes Turkey, Brazil, South Africa and India, for their dependence on foreign investment and hence vulnerability to financial market turmoil.[11] But recent assessments of the Indonesian economy have been rather upbeat.

Indonesia also fits the definition of the term "middle power", which is usually applied to countries such as Canada, Australia, the Scandinavian countries,

Japan and South Korea. Middle powers are those countries who play an active role in promoting international cooperation, and lead by ideas and example rather than by hard power, such as military strength. One Indonesian analyst argues that Indonesia is more of a middle power than say Australia or South Korea as it "is perceived as a more 'neutral' player, capable of engaging other regional players more independently".[12]

Although pitched at the global level, the focus of Indonesia has remained very much on developments in the region. Natalegawa's perception of Indonesia as a "regional power with global interests and concerns" is worth recalling in this regard.

"Independent and Active" Foreign Policy: Continuity and Change

Every nation's foreign policy and international role has a foundation, which often dates back to its beginnings as an independent nation. With some modification, it acts as the ballast for its role in world affairs. For Indonesia, it is the concept of an "independent and active" foreign policy. After gaining independence from the Dutch, Indonesian leaders characterized their foreign policy as "independent and active". In an article in *Foreign Affairs* in 1953, Mohammed Hatta, the Vice-President, wrote that as an independent nation, Indonesia would "seek friendship with all nations, whatever their ideology or form of government". He added:

> Indonesia plays no favorites between the two opposed blocs and follows its own path through the various international problems. It terms this policy "independent, " and further characterizes it by describing it as independent and "active." By active is meant the effort to work energetically for the preservation of peace and the relaxation of tension generated by the two blocs, through endeavors supported if possible by the majority of the members of the United Nations.[13]

Obviously, this approach was a response to the Cold War dynamics. Indonesia chose a path, similar to India, which had advocated a policy of non-alignment between the two power blocs. This policy was affirmed by the historic Asia-Africa Conference in 1955, hosted by Indonesia in Bandung. Another article by Hatta in *Foreign Affairs* in 1958 reiterated that policy.

> Our policy is independent and active – independent because Indonesia does
> not wish to align herself with either of the opposition blocs, the Western bloc
> or the Communist bloc; active because it actively carries out a peaceful policy
> as a loyal member of the United Nations.[14]

In that essay, Hatta also reaffirmed: "By practising her independent and active policy Indonesia endeavors to seek friendship with all nations – whatever their ideology or form of government – upon a basis of mutual respect."[15] Indonesia became a founder of the Non-Aligned Movement (NAM), an initiative that defined its approach to world order for subsequent decades.

Yet, this approach went through two important if undeclared shifts with the transition from Sukarno to Suharto in 1967. First, at the global level, while Indonesia remained committed to non-alignment, its foreign policy outlook turned more pro-Western than had been the case under Sukarno. A second important shift was a much closer advocacy of regionalism, especially regionalism in Southeast Asia in the form of ASEAN (Association of Southeast Asian Nations) which was founded in 1967.

Sukarno's foreign policy turned radical as his government faced increasing difficulties at home. Aside from visions such as the struggle between "old established forces" and "new emerging forces", Sukarno adopted a policy of Konfrontasi (confrontation) towards the newly created Malaysia. Suharto, by contrast, was a pragmatist, which was partly due to his dependence on Western support and the need to consolidate his military regime at home.

Indonesia's turn towards regionalism was the other important shift. Adam Malik, Presidium Minister for Political Affairs and Minister for Foreign Affairs, was one of the "angry young men" in his country's struggle for independence two decades earlier. As the Presidium's point man in Indonesia's efforts "to mend fences with its neighbours in the wake of an unfortunate policy of confrontation", he described Indonesia's vision of a Southeast Asia developing into "a region which can stand on its own feet, strong enough to defend itself against any negative influence from outside the region". As ASEAN's history has it, Malik viewed such a vision as "not wishful thinking if the countries of the region effectively cooperated with each other, considering their combined natural resources and manpower". Though there were "differences of outlook among the member countries", they were not irreconcilable but could be "overcome through a maximum of goodwill and understanding, faith and realism". Malik further adds that "[H]ard work, patience and perseverance...would also be necessary."[16]

The turn to regionalism was especially crucial because it helped to overcome apprehensions from its neighbour about Indonesian domination of the region which were fuelled by Sukarno's policy of Konfrontasi towards the newly formed Malaysian state during the 1963–66 period. This policy was inspired by an ideological world-view that saw the Malaysian state as a creature of British colonialism. Its end in 1966 coincided with the proposal for ASEAN which, as Michael Leifer put it, reflected a "regional vision based on an exclusive pattern of relations among resident states".[17]

The two approaches of non-alignment at the global level and regionalism at the Southeast Asian level reinforced each other. Indonesia continued to reject participation in formal alliances with great powers and sought to steer ASEAN away from an overtly pro-Western stance through initiatives such as the Zone of Peace, Freedom and Neutrality (ZOPFAN). It pushed ASEAN to develop a regional approach to peace and security so that it did not have to depend on direct military support from outside powers. That way, the region could have fewer prospects for direct intervention by the great powers.

The enduring slogan of "active and independent foreign policy" with an emphasis on region (both Southeast Asia and Asia-Pacific) thus remains an important basis of Indonesia's role as an emerging power. While this policy was never formally abandoned, with the fall of Suharto, Indonesia went into a period of unprecedented passivity.[18] Although this should not be overstated, it was clear that its foreign policy was geared more towards managing the international repercussions of domestic upheavals and issues such as the separation of East Timor. As Foreign Minister Natalegawa told this author in the immediate aftermath of the fall of Suharto, Indonesia became "inward looking" in that its foreign policy was "switched off". He called it the "opt out foreign policy". "There was a temptation to focus on national or domestic issues." "There was also the issue of trust: after East Timor, no one believed Indonesia had changed. Indonesia was also accused of being "[the] center or source of terrorism".[19]

It was the advent of Susilo Bambang Yudhoyono after Indonesia's first direct presidential elections that the country reverted its foreign policy back to "active" mode. (See Appendices 1.1 and 1.2 of this chapter.) President Yudhoyono's foreign policy reaffirmed the "independent and active" foreign policy. "The government that I lead," said the President in his first official speech after being sworn into office on 20 October 2004, "will always hold on to our free and active foreign policy. On the international stage, Indonesia will be a voice of conscience to promote peace, enhance prosperity, and stand up for justice. Indonesia will keep growing into a democratic, open, modern, pluralistic and tolerant nation."[20] Among other things, Yudhoyono's foreign policy sought to proceed by "turning liability to asset".[21] For example, whereas Indonesia was once seen as a hub of terrorism, it worked to be "seen as a hub of counter-terrorism".

At this stage, Indonesia's policy also assumed a more confident tone. Suggestive of this is President Yudhoyono's slogan of "a million friends and zero enemies".

> Indonesia is now facing a new strategic environment, where no country is regarded by Indonesia as an enemy. This way, Indonesia can freely conduct its "all directions foreign policy" where we have "a million friends and zero enemies", to build a peaceful, just, democratic, and prosperous world, above all.[22]

Before leaving Washington, D.C., the outgoing Indonesian Ambassador to the United States, Dino Patti Djalal described this foreign policy doctrine: "That means we must turn every adversary into a friend, and every friend into closer friends and even partners." He added:

> Before, the US and Indonesia were just friends, and it was all about security and counter-terrorism. But in 2010, we formed a comprehensive partnership. Basically, that means the US and Indonesia recognize that this is a strategic relationship. Now, it is broad-based and forward-looking.

Dewi Fortuna Anwar, one of the most prominent analysts of Indonesian foreign policy, who was also the chief foreign policy advisor to President Jusuf Habibie, observes that Indonesia's "free and active" foreign policy doctrine has been revitalized in the post-Cold War era:

> …Indonesia has made a special effort to revitalize its free and active foreign policy by striving to develop friendly relations with most countries while at the same time supporting a truly multilateral global power structure. President Susilo Bambang

Yudhoyono argues that Indonesia's foreign policy is characterized by the pursuit of "one million friends, zero enemies," and Foreign Minister Marty Natalegawa supports a "dynamic equilibrium" among the major powers, particularly in a regional context. Whereas the traditional concept of balance of power is conflictual in nature, the concept of dynamic equilibrium envisages a more cooperative system of relations between powers without any clear-cut adversaries."[23]

Another prominent Indonesian public intellectual, Rizal Sukma, Executive Director of the influential think-tank Centre for Strategic and International Studies (CSIS) in Jakarta, has argued that Indonesia should develop a "post-ASEAN" foreign policy outlook and role (this is discussed in Chapter 3). While ASEAN remains the cornerstone of Indonesia's foreign policy, Indonesia's focus on "region" has not been confined to Southeast Asia and ASEAN. It has expanded to engage with the wider Asia-Pacific region in the post-Cold War era. This is evident in concepts such as "geopolitics of cooperation" and "dynamic equilibrium". Both give a special emphasis to the region, encompassing both Southeast Asia and the Asia-Pacific.

A Normative Power

How do Indonesia's present leaders see their role as an emerging power? An important clue to their thinking emerges from a speech by President Yudhoyono at Wilton Park on 2 November 2012. Entitled "Indonesia's Role as a Regional and Global Actor", the speech laid special focus on the role of norms in Indonesia's approach to international order. Defining the present international situation as "a condition where Cold War tensions have been overcome, but still short from a condition of total peace", he stated:

> In such a condition, we must do our utmost to achieve an international order based on durable peace and global cooperation. Indonesia believes that this order will be peaceful, stable and sustainable if it is built upon a set of norms and principles. This is why norms setting is one of the critical parts of our foreign policy. This is why we attach particular importance to our role as a NORM SETTER (emphasis in original).[24]

President Yudhoyono went on to define Indonesia's regional and global role further in terms of being a "consensus-builder" and "peacekeeper". But arguably norm-setting remains the first and most important element of the three which are inter-related. He provided as examples of norm-setting the evolving regional code of conduct negotiations in the South China Sea and the 2011 Declaration of the East Asia Summit on the Principles of Mutually Beneficial Relations (to be discussed in Chapter 3). When attaining agreement on norms proves difficult, Indonesia would resort to consensus-building. He offered an example of this: the UN Conference on Climate Change held in Bali in 2007. When deadlock loomed in negotiations between developed and developing countries, Indonesia facilitated "intense consultations...to achieve consensus on the Bali Roadmap" where "all parties were able to agree on the Roadmap as they eventually set aside their parochial interests". As for Indonesia's role as a peacekeeper Yudhoyono saw it as "a long-standing responsibility that has been inspired by the vision of our founding fathers" and which entails an "obligation to participate in the creation of a world order based on freedom, lasting peace, and social justice".[25]

Other Indonesian leaders offer similar views. Hassan Wirajuda sees Indonesia as an "active bridge builder, not just in US-China relations but also within the East Asian community as a whole".[26] Natalegawa stresses Indonesia's role as a "moderator and facilitator" citing examples such as former Foreign Minister Ali Alatas' "cocktail diplomacy", and "Jakarta Informal Meetings" (JIM) at the height of the Cambodia conflict in the 1990s, as well as Indonesia's recent mediation role in the Southern Philippines and in the Thailand-Cambodia dispute over the Preah Vihear temple. Indeed, Indonesia is neither the richest nor the militarily most powerful country even in Southeast Asia, but it beats all other Asian nations including the major players China, Japan, and India when it comes to providing good offices and mediation. When asked why Indonesia is expected to play such a role, Natalegawa's unhesitating answer: "trust, comfort level and because bigger countries can be suffocating".[27]

Managing Great Power Relations: "Dynamic Equilibrium"

While Indonesia does not see itself as a global power, it seeks to influence the relationship among the major global powers of the 21st century (hence the evolving global order) through its role in the Asia-Pacific region (now being extended to the Indo-Pacific – a concept that signifies the inclusion of India).

This is because this region contains some of the most materially powerful actors in the contemporary international system. But how could Jakarta approach strategic relationships in this region? Obviously, it cannot do this on its own as an individual actor. Here being a regional multilateral player gives it an opening and an advantage. Multilateralism is fruitless if it simply gives primacy to the great powers, leading to the marginalization of ASEAN and thus Indonesia as the anchor of ASEAN. Indonesia's preferred approach to this challenge is "dynamic equilibrium".

The idea of "dynamic equilibrium" is a powerful example of Indonesia's regionally-based approach to global order. The term is of recent origin, but has found frequent mention in the speeches of President Yudhoyono and Foreign Minister Natalegawa. In a speech in Honolulu on 12 November 2011, the President argued that: "to anticipate the Asia-Pacific century, we need to redefine the regional architecture into an open, effective, inclusive and transparent one… the Asia Pacific century will also need to evolve a dynamic equilibrium…"[28] He elaborated the concept in a speech in Tokyo on 13 December 2013:

> "Dynamic" because change is a constant and indeed inherent in the region. The region's architecture must therefore be constantly adaptive. "Equilibrium" because such a state of constant change does not suggest a permanent state of "anarchy" or the uncertainty common to a diffuse multipolar system. Nor, on the other hand, of the imposed "order" of an unchecked preponderance of a single power. Instead, countries of the region develop norms and principles, codes of conduct, and as the case may be, legal frameworks, to build a spirit of partnership and cooperation in addressing issues of common interests.[29]

The idea of equilibrium is a modification of Indonesia's Cold War security framework known as Zone of Peace, Freedom and Neutrality (ZOPFAN), although there are some continuities. Both imply the autonomy of Southeast Asian countries over outside powers and both seek to limit their influence or interference in regional affairs. Both seek to ensure that the security of Southeast Asia is not dominated by outside powers, whether singly or collectively. However, ZOPFAN was, theoretically at least, a more exclusionary policy; it sought to deny outside powers a place or role in regional affairs. But this approach had run out of steam even before the Cold War had ended. In 1991, then Foreign Minister Ali Alatas viewed ZOPFAN as "an evolutionary process", representing "the regional, multilateral framework within which it is hoped to promote national and regional resilience and to seek the disentanglement of the region from the contending strategic designs of the great Powers".[30] To keep pace with the changing regional strategic environment, Indonesia also accepted the need for adjustments to the ZOPFAN concept.[31] As Alatas had conceded, Southeast Asian countries could not "keep the four powers [the USA, Japan, China and the Soviet Union] out of the region". The implication was that regional security would be best ensured not through excluding the great powers as envisaged in ZOPFAN, but through "equilibrium among them and between them and Southeast Asia".[32]

Indonesia's Foreign Minister since 2009, Marty Natalegawa, who is generally associated with the "dynamic equilibrium" idea, explains that it is inspired by the acute tensions that exist in the relationship among the major powers, especially in the China-US, and China-Japan relationships.[33] In addressing such tensions, the approach not only rejects the hegemony of any single power in the region, be it the United States or China, it also departs from the conventional balance of power approach. Unlike policy-makers in neighbouring Singapore, Indonesians do not like to use the term balance. Equilibrium is their preferred concept. The goal is not to create order through military build-up, alliances and arms races, but to keep ASEAN in the middle, like the "conductor in an orchestra".[34]

How to realize the policy of dynamic equilibrium? One major example of this approach was Indonesia's role in deciding the membership of the East Asia summit. In 2003, Indonesia pushed hard to have India as well as Australia and New Zealand to join the group at the outset. But the key instrument is a normative one, especially a Treaty for the Indo-Pacific region. ASEAN's Treaty of Amity and Cooperation was signed in 1976 and has initially served as a normative framework for relations among the ASEAN countries. In the early post-Cold War era, especially with the creation of the ARF in 1994, the scope of the TAC was extended to guide relations between the ASEAN countries and major outside powers. The TAC was opened to them for accession. But there is a difference between the existing TAC approach and the wider TAC conceived by Indonesia. Whereas ASEAN's current approach builds great power relations on the "ASEAN plus" formula, like China-ASEAN, or India-ASEAN, the Indo-Pacific Treaty is for the entire region. The Indo-Pacific Treaty is aimed at multilateralizing ASEAN's current hub and spoke approach to building relations among the great powers. The wider TAC is thus likened to connecting the outer dots. And it is meant not for Asia-Pacific, but the relatively new regional concept of Indo-Pacific, so "as to make sure India is there". The push for this began with Indonesia's promotion of the twelve Bali principles adopted at the East Asian Summit in 2011 in Bali. Natalegawa thinks that the principles should be given legal weight and underpinnings, or that its principles like peaceful settlement of disputes should be made legally binding. But the "modalities [of how to do this] are not yet clear". He is considering other alternative possibilities such as the African Union's permanent high council which is different from ASEAN's current provision of a High Council that convenes only when needed. Another possible model is the Antarctica Treaty.[35]

Democracy and Foreign Policy

Any framework to understand and explain Indonesia's foreign policy and role in the world has to appreciate the impact of democratization. Indonesia offers an important and reassuring example of how democratization can affect and reshape a country's foreign policy. As Natalegawa puts it, the impact of democratization on Indonesia's foreign policy is both in terms of process and substance. In terms of process, foreign policy decision-making is now "more diffuse, there is a more diverse constituency for foreign policy, a sense of public ownership and participation in the policy-making, even in post-decision [implementation] phase. It is much more important for foreign policy-makers during the dissemination phase to earn the support of the public, to get feedback, sell the policy. So overall the system is much more inclusive." In terms of substance, the impact of democratization, he argues, can be seen in Indonesia's support for democracy and human rights, including placing democracy and human rights in the ASEAN Political-Security Community, the ASEAN Charter, and its push for the ASEAN Intergovernmental Commission on Human Rights (AICHR), the creation of the Bali Democracy Forum (BDF), and Indonesia's voting in the UN Third Committee (Social, Humanitarian, Cultural Committee – that deals with humanitarian and human rights issues) on North Korea, Iran, Syria, and Myanmar, on the death penalty, and the protection of migrant workers.[36]

Democracy also serves as a check on the foreign policy authority of the executive, including the President and the Ministry of Foreign Affairs. The parliament, through the Komisi I of the lower house of the Indonesian Parliament (Dewan Perwakilan Rakyat or DPR, the People's Representative Council) which is responsible for information, defence and foreign affairs, not only vets the appointment of Indonesian ambassadors abroad, it also sometimes asserts itself against government's key foreign policy initiatives. While relations between the Parliament and the Ministry of Foreign Affairs are generally positive, the former rejected Indonesia's defence agreement with Singapore (covering extradition) because the Indonesian Government "did not explain the rationale for the treaty". On another occasion, it forced the governments hand to abstain, rather than endorse one of the UN Security Council resolutions on Iran, which the government had supported on an earlier occasion.[37] The legislature has also refused to ratify the ASEAN trans-boundary pollution agreement, which is seen by Indonesia's neighbours as a test of its commitment to curb the forest fires from Sumatra and Kalimantan that chokes Malaysia and Singapore with hazardous haze.

According to Ketut Erawan, Executive Director of the Institute of Peace and Democracy at Udayana University in Bali, which is the implementing agency of the BDF, democracy has two main functions [in foreign policy]: "it can [be] instrumental, and it can also promote identity change".[38] A country's democratic credentials can be used to address foreign policy and security challenges. For Indonesia, this has been important in persuading the US to lift sanctions against its military, which in turn allows it to buy advanced weapons to meet security threats such as terrorism. Also, democratization can bring in more development assistance and support for economic programmes. At the same time, being democratic has dramatically altered Indonesia's image in the world: Wirajuda declares, "Democracy has made Indonesia accepted by international community, both developed and developing countries, especially by the developed world."[39]

Donald K. Emmerson, a long-time and noted observer of Indonesia, aptly sums up President Yudhoyono's role:

> Yudhoyono has broadened the rationale for Indonesian involvement in foreign affairs. A case in point has been his desire to leverage his country's stature as the world's third-largest democracy — a priority that Suharto's authoritarian regime, despite calling itself a 'Pancasila democracy', could not plausibly entertain.[40]

Why does Indonesia matter to the world? Why does the rest of the world care about Indonesia? To be sure, the country's size, population, strategic location, and economic potential are important. Also important are its traditional reputation as a society that tolerates and accommodates diversity ("unity in diversity"). But the nature and purpose of its political system informing and shaping its foreign policy are also crucial. Thus, Indonesia's democracy-guided foreign policy and role, especially its role in international affairs, in ASEAN, and in the Indo-Pacific, have a major bearing on how the world looks at Indonesia and how much Indonesia matters in regional and world affairs.

While the democratic Indonesia continues to profess continuity with an active and independent foreign policy, there also have been major qualitative changes in the sources of its foreign policy. Three are especially important: democracy, development and stability.

Appendix 1.1

Tujuan/Sasaran Strategis Kementerian Luar Negeri (Purpose/Strategic Goal of Indonesia's Foreign Ministry)

1. Increase Indonesia's role and leadership in the creation of an ASEAN community in political-security, economic and socio-cultural spheres.

2. Increase Indonesia's diplomatic role in handling multilateral issues.

3. Increase cooperation in a variety of fields between Indonesia and other countries and intra-regional organizations within Asia-Pacific, Africa, the Americas, and Europe.

4. Increase the quality of international law and cooperation that is safeguarded from political, juridical, technical and security deterring factors.

5. Increase the quality of protocol and consular services.

6. Increase Indonesia's image before domestic public and the world.

7. Increase the governing quality and total diplomacy.

Appendix 1.2

Stages and Priorities of Indonesia's Foreign Policy, 2005–2025

2005–2009	Strengthen and expand national identity as a democratic country in international society
2010–2014	The recovering of Indonesia's important role as a democratic country which is marked by the success of diplomacy in international forums as a means to safeguard national security, territorial integrity, and the protection of natural resources
2015–2019	Increase the role of Indonesia as a leader and contribution in international cooperation
2020–2024	The positioning of Indonesia as an independent nation in the global community • Create market access • Position Indonesia in the right place in international rivalry • Increase foreign investment by Indonesian companies

Source: Rencana Strategis Kementerian Luar Negeri (Strategic Plan of the Ministry of Foreign Affairs), (Jakarta: Kementerian Luar Negeri, 2013).

Notes

[1] President Susilo Bambang Yudhoyono, Keynote Speech to the 7th Annual International Conference of the Overseas Private Investment Corporation (OPIC), Jakarta, 4 May 2011.

[2] Mark Landler, "Clinton Praises Indonesian Democracy", *New York Times*, 18 February 2009 <http://www.nytimes.com/2009/02/19/washington/19diplo.html?_r=0>

[3] For further discussion, see Amitav Acharya, *The End of American World Order* (Cambridge, UK: Polity Press, 2014).

[4] Santo Darmosumarto, "Indonesia and the Asia-Pacific: Opportunities and Challenges for Middle Power Diplomacy", *Policy Brief*, The German Marshall Fund of the United States (July 2013) <http://www.gmfus.org/wpcontent/blogs.dir/1/files_mf/1373398834Darmosumarto_Indonesia_Jul13.pdf>

[5] Marty Natalegawa, interview with the author, Jakarta, 20 January 2014.

[6] Acharya, *The End of American World Order*.

[7] Jim O'Neill, "Building Better Global Economic BRICS", Global Economics Paper No. 66 (New York: Goldman Sachs, 30 November 2001) <http://www.goldmansachs.com/our-thinking/topics/brics/brics-reports-pdfs/build-better-brics.pdf>. Although primarily economic in focus, the report did argue giving the BRICS a greater role in global institutions.

8   Ruchir Sharma, *Breakout Nations: In Pursuit of the Next Economic Miracles* (New York: W.W. Norton, 2012).

9   G-20 members include: Argentina, Australia, Brazil, Canada, China, European Union, France, Germany, India, Indonesia, Italy, Japan, Mexico, Russia, Saudi Arabia, South Africa, South Korea, Turkey, United Kingdom, and the United States.

10   Hassan Wirajuda, interview with the author, Jakarta, 12 March 2014. A similar view is offered by Mahendra Siregar, the G-20 "Sherpa" for Indonesia who is also the chairman of Indonesia's Investment Coordinating Board (BKPM). When asked by the author if Indonesia should seek to join the BRICS, his answer was: "I don't think so. It already has the strong ASEAN organization. ASEAN plus, so BRICS [is] not needed." Mahendra Siregar, interview with the author, Jakarta, 10 March 2014.

11   Landon Thomas Jr., "'Fragile Five' is the Latest Club of Emerging Nations in Turmoil", *New York Times*, 28 January 2014 <http://www.nytimes.com/2014/01/29/business/international/fragile-five-is-the-latest-club-of-emerging-nations-in-turmoil.html?_r=0>

12   Darmosumarto, op. cit.

13   Mohammad Hatta, "Indonesia's Foreign Policy", *Foreign Affairs*, April 1953, p. 444.

14   Mohammad Hatta, "Indonesia Between the Power Blocs", *Foreign Affairs*, April 1958.

15   Ibid. p 480.

16   "The Founding of ASEAN". <http://www.asean.org/asean/about-asean/history>

17   Michael Leifer, *Indonesian Foreign Policy* (London: Allen & Unwin, 1983), p. 181.

18   Amitav Acharya, "Is There a Lack of Focus in Indonesia's Foreign Policy", *Straits Times*, 2 October 2000.

19   Marty Natalegawa, interview with the author, Jakarta, 20 January 2014.

20   President Susilo Bambang Yudhoyono, First Inauguration Speech, 20 October 2004 (drafted by the Indonesian Embassy Washington D.C.)

21   Marty Natalegawa, interview with the author, Jakarta, 20 January 2014.

22   President Susilo Bambang Yudhoyono, First State Speech during his second term, Jakarta, 20 October 2009.

23   Dewi Fortuna Anwar, "An Indonesian Perspective on the U.S. Rebalancing Effort toward Asia". The National Bureau of Asian Research, 26 February 2013 <http://www.nbr.org/research/activity.aspx?id=320#.UyIk887DWrc>

24   President Susilo Bambang Yudhoyono, "Indonesia's role as a regional and global actor", Speech delivered at the Annual Address of Wilton Park at the Foreign and Commonwealth Office, London, 2 November 2012 <https://www.wiltonpark.org.uk/president-yudhoyonos-speech-at-our-annual-address/>

25   Ibid.

[26] Hassan Wirajuda, interview with the author, Jakarta, 12 March 2014.

[27] Marty Natalegawa, interview with the author, Jakarta, 20 January 2014.

[28] President Susilo Bambang Yudhoyono, Speech at the APEC CEO Summit, "The Asia-Pacific Century", Honolulu, Hawaii, 12 November 2011 <http://www. presidenri.go.id/index.php/eng/pidato/2011/11/13/1745.html>

[29] President Susilo Bambang Yudhoyono, Speech at the Policy Forum of the Japan Institute of International Affairs, "Building Regional Architecture for Common Peace, Stability, and Prosperity", Tokyo, 13 December 2013 <http://setkab.go.id/ pidato-11430-address-by-hh-dr-susilo-bambang-yudhoyono-president-of-the-republic-of-indonesia-at-the-policy-forum-of-the-japan-institute-of-international-affairs-tokyo-13-december-2013.html>

[30] Keynote address by Ali Alatas to the United Nations Regional Disarmament Workshop for Asia and Pacific on Disarmament (New York: United Nations Department for Disarmament Affairs, 1991), p. 14.

[31] For further discussion, see Amitav Acharya, *Constructing a Security Community in Southeast Asia: ASEAN and the Problem of Regional Order*, 1st edition (London: Routledge, 2001), p.172.

[32] "Live and Let Live", interview with Ali Alatas, Foreign Minister of Indonesia, *Far Eastern Economic Review*, 11 July 1991.

[33] Marty Natalegawa, interview with the author, Jakarta, 5 July 2011.

[34] Ibid.

[35] Marty Natalegawa, interview with the author, Jakarta, 20 January 2014.

[36] Ibid.

[37] Kemal Stamboel, a former chairman of Komisi I, interview with the author, Jakarta, 12 March 2014.

[38] Ketut Erawan, interview with the author, Denpasar, Bali, 6 January 2014.

[39] Hassan Wirajuda, interview with the author, Jakarta, 10 March 2014.

[40] Donald K. Emmerson, "Is Indonesia Rising: It Depends", in Anthony Reid, ed., *Indonesia Rising: The Repositioning of Asia's Third Giant* (Singapore: Institute of Southeast Asian Studies, 2012).

Chapter 2

DEMOCRACY, DEVELOPMENT AND STABILITY
Creating a Virtuous Cycle[1]

Unlike China and Russia, but similar to India and Brazil, Indonesia is a democratic nation. Indonesia provides some of the most striking evidence that the key to status in international affairs begins at home. When I asked him about the basis of Indonesia's foreign policy today, President Yudhoyono responded: "Progress in the domestic arena helps international role in the region and the world. To be an emerging power, a precondition is political stability, national stability."[2] Indeed, Indonesia's post-Suharto recovery and progress rests on three main domestic foundations: democracy, development and stability. Military capacity is often a critical factor behind the rise of nations, but in Indonesia's case, it is yet to be important, and unlikely to be important for some time. While economic development is often regarded as the passport to a country's success, Indonesians for the time being are more proud of their democracy. Moreover, it can be argued that a country's status or image in today's world is better ensured with all three elements present. As President Yudhoyono explains, "While outsiders focus on economic progress, the real achievement [of Indonesia] is democracy, and harmonizing democracy, development, Islam and human rights."[3]

The Suharto era was recognized by some for its economic growth and stability, but not democracy. Singapore, which enjoys both development and stability, is less pluralistic than post-Suharto Indonesia. Thailand, which has enjoyed a reasonable degree of economic development, has suffered from chronic instability and a breakdown of democracy, as evident in the 2006 and 2014 military coups. Indonesia might join the ranks of South Korea, perhaps the only other nation aside from highly developed Japan that currently enjoys all three aspects – democracy, development, and internal stability – in good measure.

Moreover, Indonesia shows that the impact of the three elements could be inter-related in a virtuous cycle. Democratization has fostered internal stability, which in turn has promoted economic development. Economic development and internal stability have supported the legitimization of the political system, and the consolidation of democracy.

Indonesia's domestic arena challenges some powerful myths about the relationship among democracy, development and stability. The first is that democracy is somehow inimical to development. As President Yudhoyono states, "In the past, there was a sense that countries had to choose between the two [democracy and development], but Indonesia has proven to the world that the two can go together."[4] With a growth rate above those of the other BRICS, save China and India, and an economy projected to be among the top ten in the world, Indonesia demolishes the view popularized by the economic successes of South Korea, Taiwan, and China that authoritarian rule is needed to promote economic development.

Indonesia also challenges a popular view among academics and analysts that newly democratic states are more likely to suffer from greater internal strife, turn rabidly nationalistic, and seek war with their neighbours. As Indonesia entered a new era of stable democratic governance and regional leadership, it silenced critics of democratization who blame quick democratic transitions for internal violence and foreign adventurism. Indonesia also shows that contrary to the popular suspicion that Islam is an inhospitable condition for democracy, Islam and democracy can go hand-in-hand.

Democratization in Indonesia has not been free from violence. The world had reason to doubt that Indonesia would be able to manage a democracy – after all, Suharto had been president for thirty-three years at the time of his downfall. Widespread riots accompanied the weeks before and after Suharto's downfall. Thousands of people lost their lives. But the past three general elections (both parliamentary and presidential), including the 2014 parliamentary and presidential elections have been free of violence.

Democratization has been a key factor behind Indonesia's ability to foster greater internal stability by resolving the long-standing conflicts in East Timor and Aceh. Subsequent measures of decentralization have helped to foster greater national stability. And Indonesia has done a far better job than anyone had expected in managing the threat posed by radicalism and terrorism in the wake of the 9/11 attacks on the US and in Indonesia itself.

After Suharto was forced to resign from office in May 1998, Reformasi fever reached virtually every segment of Indonesian society. Islamist scholars and secular technocrats, cosmopolitan elites and the village poor, have all accepted the need for democratic change. A combination of economic growth and political reform has made Indonesia stronger than ever within Southeast Asia – Indonesia is not only the region's largest economy but an enthusiastic yet non-aggressive, promoter of political liberalism.

Democratization

The new Indonesia is the direct result of its consolidating democracy. Indonesia's 1945 Constitution was amended four times in order to compromise between reformists who wanted to create an entirely new Constitution and conservatives who wanted to keep the Constitution as is. In 1999, the Constitution was amended to put term limits (two terms) on the president and vice-president and give the People's Representative Council (DPR, the Lower House of Parliament), rather than the President, sole legislative powers.[5] In 2000, the Constitution was amended to make the president more accountable to the DPR, make the DPR and the provincial and district assemblies (DPRDs) fully-elected through direct elections, remove military and police representation in these bodies, and add ten human rights provisions, including freedom of religion, freedom of movement, the right to protection from discriminatory treatment, and the right to private property without arbitrary interference. Freedom of expression is guaranteed as well, though subject to prevailing law. Provinces and regions were given a greater role, with regions allowed to act on any issue not expressly assigned to the central government and Parliament allowed to pass special autonomy laws for particular provinces.

The third constitutional amendment, passed in 2001, created the Regional Representative Council (DPD), a legislative chamber tasked with discussing bills pertaining to regions. Like the DPR, the DPD is directly-elected, but unlike DPR parliamentarians, DPD representatives do not need to be associated with parties. A Judicial Commission was also created to oversee judges, including those of the Supreme Court and Constitutional Court. In the fourth and final amendment in 2002, the structure of Parliament was re-arranged. The MPR, which previously included DPR parliamentarians and members of functional groups, now consists solely of the 560 members of the DPR and the 132 members of the DPD. It is responsible for passing constitutional amendments and if necessary, impeaching presidents. Additionally, a Constitutional Court was created, and soon given the power of judicial review over legislation passed after the first constitutional amendment.

Direct parliamentary elections, introduced through the Second Amendment, were first implemented in the 2004 election. Direct presidential elections, introduced through the Fourth Amendment, began in 2004. Voter participation in each of Indonesia's elections has been high. Voter turnout has decreased from 93.3 per cent in 1999 to 70.99 per cent in 2009, as is typical for democratizing states.[6] In the most recent parliamentary election, however, preliminary results suggest that voter turnout actually increased to 73 per cent.[7]

A law on political parties passed in 1999 allowed more than three parties to exist and freed them from the obligation to have the Pancasila as their base ideology (although most political parties in practice list either the Pancasila or Islam as their core). The independent General Elections Commission (KPU) was also created in time for the 1999 elections. Previous to 2004, voters could pick parties but the parties determined the representatives they would send to Parliament. For the 2004 elections, however, voting became open-list instead of closed-list, prompting increased intra-party competition and a much more direct democracy. Direct local elections were expanded along with the Regional Autonomy Law. Also in conjunction with the regional autonomy initiative, the old Upper House of Parliament (MPR) was converted to encompass the entire legislative branch, while a new legislative body, the Regional Representative Council (DPD), took its place as the "upper house". The DPD's 132 members need not be tied to parties and are tasked with discussing issues related to regional autonomy, although Indonesians are not necessarily aware of the DPD and only recently was the DPD given the power to propose bills to the DPR. And most importantly, direct presidential elections – instead of appointment by the upper house of Parliament (MPR) – were added to the Constitution in 2002.[8]

To be elected, the winning candidate must win a majority of the vote (in two rounds if necessary), along with 20 per cent of the vote in over half the nation's provinces to ensure that the new president has a wide enough base of support. Yudhoyono was the first president to have been elected by actually passing these hurdles (Jusuf Habibie was appointed; Abdurrahman Wahid and Sukarnoputri Megawati both gained office through their parties' power deals) and as such seemed to have a popular mandate. While the pace of reform slowed somewhat in his second term, it must be recalled that Indonesia has placed a high priority on maintaining a system of checks and balances in its central government in order to avoid a repeat of its authoritarian past. While parliamentary deadlock and political compromise are frustrating to reformists, these are practically inevitable facts of life in a democratic system. The fact that Indonesia has so far maintained political openness and resisted the urge to circumvent the democratic system in the name of decisive leadership has been crucial to its democratic consolidation.

The 2009 Indonesian elections showed declining support for Islamic parties, who, many in the West had mistakenly feared, could take the nation down on a spiral of extremism and violence. Their share of votes declined from 38.1 per cent in the 2004 elections to 27.8 per cent in the 2009 elections, the poorest showing ever by Islamic parties in a democratic election in Indonesia. This decline has been attributed to several factors: corruption scandals that have tainted Islamic parties' self-ascribed moral high ground (particularly the Prosperous Justice Party, PKS), the perception that Islamic parties do not have the broad-based platform necessary to provide solutions to Indonesia's problems, a rejection of extremist platforms, and secular-nationalist parties' attempts to incorporate Islam into their platforms, thereby weakening the appeal of a purely Islamic party. In the recent 2014 parliamentary elections Islamic parties have received a higher-than-expected percentage of the vote – between 31 and 32 per cent.[9] It should be noted, however, that Islamic parties appear to have gained traction because of their centrist platforms, strong organization and mobilization, and spending on social programmes.[10]

A second area of change in Indonesia's democracy is decentralization. Facing anxieties both internally and abroad that Indonesia would be "the next Yugoslavia", and encouraged by civil society voices and pro-democracy advisers, Suharto's successor Habibie embarked on a bold decentralization agenda. The 1999 Regional Autonomy Law, implemented two years later, gave municipal and district governments a greater role in governance – provincial governments were by-passed for fear that autonomy at that level would fuel separatism.[11]

Sub-national governments were not only allowed to keep more of their tax and natural resource revenues, but were also given additional funds from the central government with which to administer their populations.[12] Provincial and district governments now receive over 60 per cent of Indonesia's total domestic tax revenue.[13] Although demand for regional autonomy was strong, not all regional governments were equipped to take over the national government's role, particularly on the provision of social services.[14]

Local governments have not necessarily made the wisest policy decisions with their newfound power. In many cases, business regulations have been excessive – exacerbating local elite corruption.[15] Decentralization has also frequently led to confusion about proper jurisdiction, as lower-level governments have often enacted more radical local provisions on issues that only the national government should have authority over (particularly in religious affairs, i.e., the implementation of sharia law).[16] Despite these problems, decentralization deserves credit for increasing the accountability of politicians and empowering innovative local leaders to promote substantive change.[17]

Increased civil liberties are another notable aspect of Indonesia's democratization. While some colonial anti-treason laws remain in the Criminal Code, and in 2007 the government banned provincial separatist flags,[18] overall, political freedoms have greatly increased since the beginning of Reformasi. Press liberalization – and a corresponding flourishing of social media[19] – is the most striking example. Since the Habibie presidency, political prisoners have mainly become a thing of the past. The propagandistic Ministry of Information was eliminated by President Wahid. It would appear that the political space for defining one's own "Indonesianness" has expanded, as long as loyalty to the Indonesian unitary state remains firm.

Indonesia's concern for political freedoms has at times even complicated its foreign policy and national security requirements. Newly democratic Indonesia refused to ban the Jemaah Islamiyah (JI) organization or adopt legislation, similar to the Internal Security Acts (ISAs) of Singapore and Malaysia, to fight terrorism. Members of the Indonesian Parliament and civil society organizations vigorously opposed such a move, drawing parallels with the repressive laws and practices of the Suharto regime.

Indonesia's democratic transformation has received international recognition. In a 10 November 2010 speech at the University of Indonesia, US President

Barrack Obama noted Indonesia's "extraordinary democratic transformation – from the rule of an iron fist to the rule of the people". He also praised the resilience of Indonesia's democratic transition: "just as your democracy is symbolized by your elected President and legislature, your democracy is sustained and fortified by its checks and balances: a dynamic civil society; political parties and unions; a vibrant media and engaged citizens who have ensured that – in Indonesia – there will be no turning back from democracy".[20] Larry Diamond, a noted expert on democratic transitions, wrote in 2009: "Indonesia is doing better today than any of the democracies that lost democracy were at the time they lost it." Diamond further pointed out that Indonesians gave an average score of 7 out of 10 (with 10 being "most democratic") when asked to what extent they think their country is a democracy, and an 8.5 out of 10 when asked to what extent they want their country to be a democracy. Diamond concluded that Indonesia is doing better compared to five other surveyed Asian countries (South Korea, Taiwan, Thailand, Philippines and Mongolia): "Looking in historical terms, and in comparative terms, what Indonesia has achieved in the last 10 years (in terms of the development and improvement of democratic institutions, a critical and substantial base of public support for democracy, of trust in public institutions, and, surprisingly perhaps, robust support for liberal values relative to elsewhere in the region) is quite remarkable and is deserving of admiration."[21]

In one of the best studies of the subject, Donald Horowitz argues that Indonesia's democratization was successful in large part because it defied the conventional wisdom: most boldly, it held elections before undergoing constitutional change, placing the highest premium on immediately providing Indonesians with political choice. The resulting reform process was therefore dominated by political elite insiders, incremental, and coloured with compromise. In addition, multipolar fluidity and a fragmented party system have worked to smooth over rather than exacerbate dangerous social cleavages. Indonesia, therefore, presents an unusual success story – one that may well be worth learning from.[22]

Despite the overall progress, challenges remain. One is the quality of Indonesia's democracy. Some analysts view the Indonesian democracy as being of "low" quality. Phillips Vermonte of the Centre for Strategic and International Studies says that "democratic institutions" and the "culture of democracy" are two different issues, like "[the] chicken and [the] egg". He distinguishes between "procedural" democracy (institutions) and "substantive" democracy (democratic culture), and argues that while the former is working well in Indonesia, the latter remains weak. However, he expects substantive democracy to come later; thanks to Indonesia's diversity, the "learning period in Indonesia is longer".[23] Ignas Kleden, a sociologist and the Chairman of the Indonesian Community for Democracy (KID), noted that "of the 550 members of parliament, there are no more than 40 percent who are able to engage in substantial debates about the issues under discussion. The remaining 60 percent can only be involved in the debates about their parties' position, but can offer no contribution whatsoever to the substance of the debate."[24]

Another challenge is combatting corruption. Indonesia's scores in Transparency International's Corruption Perceptions Index have improved since 1998.[25] After reaching a low of 17 in 1999–2000, Indonesia's CPI score had lifted to 32 in 2012–13. Its global ranking was 114 in 2013. This is an improvement over its poor 2007 ranking of 143. (See Figure 2.1)

In 2002, Indonesia created its lead national anti-corruption agency, the Corruption Eradication Commission (Komisi Pemberantasan Korupsi, or KPK). The KPK is internationally-recognized for its extraordinary zeal in prosecuting corrupt "big fish" in government and politics. KPK attracts a great deal of publicity and parties have sought to use it as a political tool – to little avail. The KPK has prosecuted several high-ranking officials of the ruling Democratic Party (including Muhaimin Iskandar, Muhammad Nazaruddin, Andi Mallarangeng, and Anas Urbaningrum, among others). The Democrats are not alone – graft cases tried by KPK also brought down the formerly flashy Prosperous Justice Party, an Islamic party that had campaigned on the basis of being clean. Some conservative factions of parliament have repeatedly tried to curtail KPK's powers, particularly its ability to carry out wire-tapping and indictment (in 2008 and again in 2014). Attempts have also been made to reduce KPK's budget, downsize its facilities, and imprison two of its commissioners on ironic corruption charges (in 2009). Yet each time, the public has rallied behind KPK.[26]

Corruption allegations have touched even the perceived "good guys" of Indonesian government – Akil Mokhtar was arrested in October 2013 for accepting bribes related to the resolution of election disputes while he was

Figure 2.1

**Indonesia's Transparency International Corruption
Perceptions Index Scores**

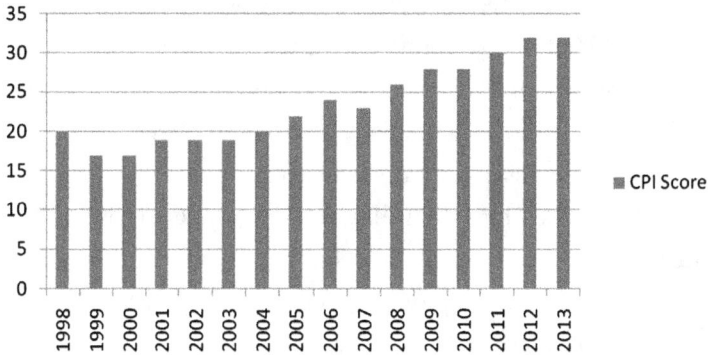

the sitting chief justice of the Constitutional Court. The KPK's nearly-perfect conviction rate should be seen in the context that it can only take on a tiny fraction of the corruption cases that are reported to the organization. Still, Indonesian anti-corruption efforts are making progress. In the future, Indonesia must not only continue to support the KPK but also support comprehensive initiatives to reduce the risk factors for corruption: official monopoly power over a good or service, total discretion over the distribution of that good or service, and a lack of accountability regarding this decision-making process.[27]

As noted in the previous chapter, Indonesia's democratization has had a direct impact on its foreign policy. Moreover, it has had a demonstration effect on its neighbours, Malaysia's own Reformasi movement being a case in point. Even more significant is Myanmar's political and economic liberalization–especially since both states have multi-ethnic populations and a history of military involvement in politics, Indonesia has frequently been cited as a model that Myanmar can learn from.[28] Indeed, Myanmar's military junta based their nation's constitution on Indonesia's original 1945 Constitution. Today, Myanmar's reformists also look to their counterparts in Indonesia. The United States – perhaps the world's most prominent advocate of democracy – also recognizes Indonesia's potential to reach out to closed states that US policies cannot influence. Indonesia's low-key approach to democracy promotion through sharing of lessons and helping with institutions may prove in some cases to be more effective.

Development

By some accounts Indonesia is the 10th largest economy in the world, up from 16th position, and the largest in Southeast Asia. According to the *Jakarta Post* in its article "RI 10th largest economy, WB", on 5 May 2014, while Indonesia was earlier ranked as the 16th largest economy in the world, according to a recent report by the International Comparison Program (ICP), which is supported by the World Bank, Indonesia had become the world's 10th largest economy by 2011, after the United States, China. India, Japan, Germany, Russia, Brazil, France, and the United Kingdom. Indonesia's GDP has grown at a rate comparative to the BRICS states, at an average clip of 5.4 per cent between 2000 and 2013 – and above 6 per cent in 2008, 2010, 2011, and 2012 – thanks to increased labour productivity and a growing labour force.[29]

Fortunately, the Indonesian economy has actually been able to produce enough jobs (1.2 million in 2012) to keep this work-force occupied.[30] The unemployment rate has declined steadily from 8.4 per cent in 2008 to 6.1 per cent in 2012. Most of this economic growth has been in the area of domestic consumption (60 per cent) and services, not exports – a fact that has protected Indonesia from being overly-vulnerable to the whims of global demand. This domestic dynamic corresponds to the aforementioned growth in a young and increasingly urban labour force eager to benefit materially from their entrance into the working world – a more moderate version of the transformation that will take place over the next decade in China and India.[31] There are 45 million middle-class Indonesians, and McKinsey & Company predicts an additional 90 million by 2030.[32] These new consumers will need to be catered to, via greater technological distribution across the country and the daunting task of sweeping the political system free of corruption.

The Asian Financial Crisis in 1997 severely affected Indonesia, due to corporate debts in US dollars and a quickly depreciating rupiah following the free-fall of the Thai baht. The three IMF agreements that Suharto was forced to accept in the twilight of his presidency were painful – the rupiah was allowed to float, the banking sector was restructured, sixteen banks were forcibly closed, public subsidies were reduced, state-owned companies put on public sale, and Suharto's crony-run monopolies taken apart.[33] Considering that the crisis left Indonesia mired in debt (government debt was 70 per cent of Indonesia's

Table 2.1

BRICS and Indonesia: Annual Growth Rates, 1998–2012

	1998	1999	2000	2001	2002	2003	2004	2005	2006	2007	2008	2009	2010	2011	2012
Brazil	0	0.3	4.3	1.3	2.7	1.1	5.7	3.2	4	6.1	5.2	-0.3	7.5	2.7	0.9
Russia	-5.3	6.4	10	5.1	4.7	7.3	7.2	6.4	8.2	8.5	5.2	-7.8	4.5	4.3	3.4
India	6.2	8.8	3.8	4.8	3.8	7.9	7.9	9.3	9.3	9.8	3.9	8.5	10.5	6.3	3.2
China	7.8	7.6	8.4	8.3	9.1	10	10.1	11.3	12.7	14.2	9.6	9.2	10.4	9.3	7.8
South Africa	0.5	2.4	4.2	2.7	3.7	2.9	4.6	5.3	5.6	5.5	3.6	-1.5	3.1	3.5	2.5
Indonesia	-13.1	0.8	4.9	3.6	4.5	4.8	5	5.7	5.5	6.3	6	4.6	6.2	6.5	6.2

Source: World Bank, World Development Indicators.

GDP at the time of the crisis, but was down to 24 per cent in 2012, when its credit rating was raised to investment grade by both Fitch and Moody's[34]) and suffering from inflation (now down to 8 per cent from 20 per cent), Indonesia's economic transformation is particularly worth noting.[35]

Suharto was left in a very weak position by the crisis and its aftermath – he dragged his feet on implementing the IMF reforms, and the loss of economic stability cost Suharto his political credibility as well. After his resignation, the technocrats in charge of the Indonesian economy were able to incorporate economic reforms into the wider (socio-political) Reformasi programme. They took a conservative approach to macroeconomic fundamentals, and the economy eventually stabilized. Though Megawati made little headway in political reform, her technocratic economic team did bring Indonesia's economy out of IMF indebtedness by implementing tough fiscal discipline.[36]

Indonesian economists have refrained from tooting their own horn – Gita Wirjawan, the former Trade Minister, demurred from answering the question of whether Indonesia belongs with the BRICS by saying Indonesia does not want a status it does not deserve.[37] But the international community has taken note of Indonesia's strong performance. As noted in Chapter 1, Indonesia is not part of the BRICS, though it has been favourably compared with them.[38] Indonesia is also included in other projections of future economic success: Goldman Sachs' "Next 11", PricewaterhouseCoopers' "E-7" (Emerging 7), *The Economist's* "CIVETS" (Colombia, Indonesia, Vietnam, Egypt, Turkey and South Africa), and Citigroup's "3G".[39]

In comparison to the BRICS countries in 2012, Indonesia's total investment as a percentage of GDP, gross national savings, and inflation rate were second only to China. Indonesia is lacking in comparison to other BRICS countries in terms of unemployment and government revenue raised, though it also spends a great deal less than the other BRICS states. Indonesia was ranked fifth in a list of emerging markets that promised long-term success for the 2012–17 period in a survey of top executives.[40] The Jakarta Index has closely trailed the S&P 500, in spite of vulnerability due to most of the listed companies being commodities companies.[41] Global economic and political conditions have also improved in Indonesia's favour – the United States Federal Reserve began quantitative easing and increased monetary flow to emerging markets in 2008, the Global

Table 2.2
BRICS and Indonesia: Economic Indicators, 2012

	Population (mn)	GDP World Ranking	GDP per capita (current US$ bn)	Total investment (% GDP)	Gross national savings (% GDP)	Inflation, average consumer prices (% change)	Unemployment rate (% total labour force)	General government revenue (% GDP)	General government total expenditure (% GDP)
Brazil	198.361	7	11,359	17.637	15.23	5.404	5.5	37.672	40.351
Russia	141.924	8	14,302	24.908	28.593	5.068	6	37.437	37.021
India	1,227.19	10	1,501	35.616	30.829	10.436		19.355	27.326
China	1,354.04	2	6,071	48.854	51.203	2.65	4.1	22.669	24.861
South Africa	51.069	28	7,525	19.414	13.152	5.654	25.125	27.907	32.7
Indonesia	244.468	16	3,594	35.324	32.584	4.259	6.14	18.032	19.689

Source: International Monetary Fund, World Economic Outlook Database, October 2013.

Financial Crisis largely left Indonesia unscathed, and as China and India lead the way in new consumers, the Indonesian economy was well-positioned to fill these states' demand for coal, palm oil, and commodities.[42]

Indonesia is projected to have the potential to be the world's seventh largest economy by 2030.[43] However, pushing through the economic reforms necessary to achieve this goal may be a challenge. Any reformers in the Finance Ministry must contend with a formidably strong Parliament that tends to be responsive to – and in some cases, responsible for – reactionary populist rhetoric. And unlike political reforms intended to hold politicians accountable to the people and increase the rights of citizens, economic reforms seldom have the popular backing necessary to overcome vested interests.

Jacob Nuwa Wea, a former union leader who took advantage of post-1998 political openness and entered politics with PDI-P, became Megawati's Minister for Manpower and Transmigration. Nuwa Wea's career epitomizes the compromises that the new democratic era created – he could be accused of having his activism co-opted by a political party, but he could also be credited with "co-opting" state power to better protect Indonesian labourers. In 2003, he pushed forward a new labour law that introduced broad protections and benefits for workers, while at the same time allowing for more flexible contracts that could benefit employers. The government tried to change the law in 2006 to lower labour costs, but unions successfully staged demonstrations to protect the law.[44]

Ordinary Indonesians have benefited from national economic growth. Gross national income per capita has increased from US$2,200 in 2000 to US$3,563 in 2012.[45] Indonesia continues to struggle with inequality, which can pose a serious risk to political longevity in such a populous democracy. The World Bank estimates that half of all households reside near the poverty line ($22/month). The government still under-invests in educating its young work-force (spending 3 per cent of its GDP on education), explaining in large part why the supply of skilled labour (55 million in 2012) is not as high as it needs to be.[46] Rice, healthcare, and education subsidies have all featured in post-Suharto economic policies. In 2013, Jakarta Governor Joko "Jokowi" Widodo put a popular universal healthcare system into action in Jakarta. If he becomes president in 2014, he will likely try to extend this system nationwide.

The budget exists for such a social safety net – indeed, the Indonesian budget usually suffers from poorly-planned underspending that must be sloppily rectified at the end of the fiscal year. Indonesian leaders have emphasized the importance of innovation if Indonesia is to be globally-competitive, and investing in Indonesia's 250 million people is crucial to creating an environment that is conducive to innovation.

On the other hand, expensive fuel subsidies have been a repeated point of political contention – they might do more to help the middle and upper-classes than the poor, but large populist demonstrations are held whenever the government tries to cut them – but against all odds the Yudhoyono government has successfully raised fuel prices three times (2005, 2008, and 2013). With each fuel price increase, the riots have shrunk – indicating that perhaps Indonesians are growing to accept that such fuel subsidies are unfeasible. Extolling Indonesia's natural resource dividend is common rhetorical practice, but in fact, mining, oil, and gas make up only about 11 per cent of Indonesia's nominal GDP.[47] Indonesian policymakers will need to ensure that the country's energy and resource policy is able to keep up with the demands of its growing consumer class – to avoid an unsustainable dependence on oil imports, Indonesia will need to pursue alternative energy sources and build more energy-efficient infrastructure.[48]

Indonesia also continues to struggle with infrastructure investment. In every area, including land and sea transportation, electricity, and water management, poor infrastructure leads to increased production costs. This not only hinders the maximization of foreign investment, but also regional connectivity across the archipelago – basic commodities are often overpriced in islands far from Java. In 2014, Indonesia was ranked 53rd in the World Bank's Logistics Performance Index – it is an improvement from 2010, when it ranked 75th, but its current ranking still places it below Malaysia, Thailand, and Vietnam.[49] If Indonesia wants to meet the goals of its current Masterplan for Acceleration and Expansion of Indonesia's Economic Development (MP3EI) – efficient production and well-integrated, competitive domestic markets – domestic policy-makers will need to gather the political will to prioritize infrastructural investment. Yudhoyono's government recognized this, and some positive moves in this direction have been made – including a 2011 land acquisition law that should accelerate the completion of government road, seaport, and airport projects.[50]

Foreign investors would have enthusiastically assisted in infrastructure development. But they have received mixed signals from the Indonesian Government, complicated by the fact that decentralization multiplied the layers of government bureaucracy that must be sifted through to receive approval for any project. Foreign investors were welcomed back to Indonesia during Yudhoyono's first term, which coupled with rising commodity prices to bolster the aforementioned high annual growth rates.[51] However, maintaining a balance between encouraging and controlling foreign investment has been a push-and-pull process. The Investment Negative List was revised in December 2013 to increase the amount of foreign investment permitted in pharmaceutical companies, advertising agencies, and power plants, though proposals to expand limits to foreign investment in oil and gas, transportation, and education were dropped.[52] While the 2007 Investment Law gives domestic and foreign investors equal legal status, it also includes a long list of sectors from which FDI is banned or heavily restricted.[53]

Foreign investors are worried about protectionist legislation, particularly as it concerns Indonesia's natural resources, which are considered to be national assets. This has seriously worried the international investor community. The Indonesian regulatory system is opaque and confusing to foreign investors. Commercial courts have made some disturbing and damaging judgments against foreign companies' local branches (for example, the Indonesian branch of the British company Prudential), though some rulings have been overturned upon appeal.[54] The 2009 Mining Law subjected foreign mining companies to the confusing administrative whims of local governments, placed time limits on their ownership of Indonesian mines, and required them to increase value-added processing without providing support for the capital investment this adjustment would require.[55]

A law put into force in January 2014 bans nickel and bauxite exports and enacts a progressive export tax on other raw-mineral exports, forcing mining companies to build smelters in Indonesia and export higher-value-added products instead. Although the ban was originally slated to include copper, this mineral was spared – apparently to accommodate American companies Freeport McMoRan Copper & Gold and Newport Mining Group, which continue to negotiate with the government on the issue of the export tax and the requirement to build smelters. This is, after all, the major intent of the law: more domestic smelters, not fewer exports.[56]

The ban is in keeping with Indonesia's MP3EI for 2011–14, which emphasizes value-adding in industrial production, as well as Indonesia's long-term economic vision of shifting economic priority from agriculture and extractive industries to high-value-added products. Fortunately for Indonesia, the laws supporting this economic vision have yet to significantly dampen foreign investment. Indonesia remains Southeast Asia's largest economy, with a young and eager workforce, a growing consumer class, and an increasingly stable and secure political environment. Aside from the dip in foreign direct investment following the 2008 Global Financial Crisis, realized FDI has increased each year, from US$6.0 billion in 2006 to US$24.6 billion in 2012. Total investment reached US$9 billion in July 2013.[57]

Stability

Indonesia did not transition peacefully into a democratic system. It took months of domestic turbulence during 1998, marked by not only extensive property damage and looting in major cities but also violence and bodily injury, death and sexual assault. The main victims of Reformasi were the Chinese-Indonesians (mostly of the working and middle classes), a group that has historically been scapegoated for a variety of social ills. In the 1960s, it was Communism; in 1998, it was the economic plight of "ordinary" Indonesians. But compared to the transition into the Suharto regime, which was accompanied by the deaths of hundreds of thousands, the damage wrought by the transition into a democratic system was relatively limited. Even anti-Chinese violence has greatly reduced since this final orgy of violence in 1998 – it has been suggested that it was Suharto's New Order that placed Chinese-Indonesians in such an ambiguous social role of economic power coupled with political weakness that the group became vulnerable to collective violence.[58] Still, fears that Indonesia was descending down a dark path of social instability dogged the country for several years. While the outbreak of violence in a country that foreign investors had assumed to be secure and stable was shocking to many, it should be recalled when comparing Indonesian stability in the pre-Suharto and post-Suharto periods that the previous regime used a great deal of state-sponsored "hidden" violence. This includes violence against suspected criminals, separatists and political dissidents.

The most violent conflicts in the immediate years following Reformasi were sectarian in nature, fought along ethnic and religious identity lines. These identities were activated and mobilized by a repeated history of economic grievances, usually the result of official government policies, for example, transmigration from overpopulated islands like Java to outer islands focused on natural resource extraction. As the result of a 1974 law, moreover, traditional village leaders had their authority reduced in the bureaucratic hierarchy.[59] In each case, tension and smaller incidents had steadily built over several decades until an "outbreak" triggered by a relatively minor incident – a street brawl or a burned home – erupted during the uncertainty and sudden "openness" of Reformasi.

One early conflict, beginning in 1997, was centred in Poso, a town in the province of Central Sulawesi. The province was declared a transmigration destination in 1973, and Muslims from South Sulawesi moved into areas traditionally dominated by local Christians. Between 1,000 and 2,500 died in the conflict, and 100,000 were displaced. Because Poso is near the Philippines, the conflict lured militant Muslim separatists based across the maritime border in Mindanao. The terrorist network Jema'ah Islamiyah and militant Muslim group Laskar Jihad also became involved. In 2001, a ceasefire was arranged through the government's Malino I Agreement (spearheaded by future leaders Susilo Bambang Yudhoyono and Jusuf Kalla).[60] This agreement included returning property to its pre-conflict owners, collecting weapons, and repatriating 90,000 refugees. However, the agreement was widely disseminated at the grassroots level on both sides of the conflict, joint commissions were established to address law and order and inequality concerns, and US$10 million was provided for rehabilitation.[61]

Violence in Ambon, in the province of Maluku, began on 19 January 1999. Ambon has historically been evenly divided between Muslims and Christians, but the arrival of migrants from Sulawesi in the 1970s–1980s shifted the equilibrium to favour the Muslim community (both local and migrant), and Muslims began getting jobs that would have ordinarily gone to Christians. The militant Muslim group Laskar Jihad, with the tacit support of some high-ranking government officials, eventually sent trained fighters to Ambon, thus tipping the conflict decidedly in favour of the Muslims. The northern Maluku conflict based on the island of Halmahera began several months later, on 18 August 1999 – several months before North Maluku was scheduled to become its own province. Again, it broke down along Muslim-Christian lines, and again, it stemmed from economic anxiety: a gold mine was discovered in the district of Malifut, and both the Muslim and Christian communities sought to control it.[62]

In total, 5,000 people were killed and an additional 500,000 were displaced in Maluku. A state of emergency was declared in June 2000, and the Malino II Agreement peace deal was signed in 2002 (again led by Kalla). Malino II followed the outlines of its Poso predecessor but also included investigations into human rights violations and more specific instructions for preparing military, police, and public institutions to fairly execute their duties.[63] Like the Malino I Agreement, it was criticized for being a top-down process with minimal participation.[64] Due to inconsistent implementation, sporadic violence has continued in Maluku in the years that followed. Community-based interfaith initiatives, however, helped reintegrate the divided communities.[65]

In the West and Central Kalimantan provinces, Madurese migrants were attacked by the indigenous Dayak people in the districts of Sambas and Sampit in 1999 and 2001, respectively, in a follow-up to a similar 1996 attack. The Madurese had relocated to Kalimantan as part of a transmigration programme initiated by the Dutch colonists in the 1930s, and continued by the Suharto regime. The transmigrants were given legal control over various lucrative industries, sowing resentment among the Dayaks. Beginning with the 1996 attacks, roughly 1,000 were killed. Although President Wahid had visited the area to put pressure on both sides to cease fighting, the state played a limited role in the resolution of this conflict, and 70,000 Madurese fled back to Madura.[66] Instead, civil society networks led the conflict resolution effort following the 2001 riots.

These examples of civilian communal violence and *massa aksi* (mass action), which became a popular phenomenon nationwide, illustrate the state's loss of monopoly on violence after the Reformasi movement of 1998. In democratic Indonesia, the state no longer attempts to manipulate particular sub-groups in an effort to control the social order. This does not mean that Indonesia has become less stable since democratization. Indeed, much of the violence in the democratic period has its roots in Suharto's New Order policies.[67] These roots include political oppression, inter-ethnic manipulation, preferential economic policies, and transmigration, among others. Indeed, some of the most deadly conflicts of the early democratic years, for example, the conflict between the Madurese and the Dayak in Central Kalimantan, which began in December 1996 – started in the twilight of the New Order.[68]

Internal violence, previously a serious threat to stability across Indonesia, has declined sharply. The number of violent incidents, as tracked by the Habibie Center's National Violence Monitoring System (NVMS, or Sistem Nasional Pemantauan Kekerasan [SNPK]) in a sample of nine conflict-prone provinces,[69] has actually remained more or less at the same level – 1,229 incidents in 1999, and 1,193 incidents in 2013. In terms of property damage and lives lost, however, conflicts have become much less dangerous. Following a high of 4,184 deaths from violence in 1999, the number of deaths has dropped to 141 in 2013. The number of buildings damaged has plummeted from a high of 18,540 in 2000 to 601 in 2013. These numbers indicate that while tensions and grievances continue to fester in the Indonesian archipelago, the resulting outburst of such tensions has become much less volatile. Data shows that local conflicts, which sometimes pit entire villages against each other, have usually correlated with unemployment, inequality, natural disasters, changes in income sources, inward and outward migration, and ethnic group clusters within villages.[70] These findings would indicate that internal violence in Indonesia has been a side-effect of a country in transition. As local conditions change and old social structures meet with upheaval, communal violence becomes a way to resolve conflict and correct grievances. It may also be reasonable to infer that as Indonesia's socio-economic development and national stability have been maintained, the triggers for these conflicts have been reduced.

Unsurprisingly, the high mark of internal conflicts was passed in the immediate chaos of Reformasi, although separatist conflicts remained flammable before flat-lining after 2005, when the Helsinki Peace Agreement on Aceh was reached. Data reveals that identity conflicts, while worrisome in the initial post-Suharto years, have also sharply reduced since 2002. The incidence of conflict based in resources, governance, or elections has risen mildly between 1999 and 2013. Conflict related to popular justice, however, had increased from 147 incidents in 1999 to 510 incidents in 2013.

Popular justice in this case refers to civilians taking the law into their own hands in pursuit of a suspected criminal or other social transgressor. At times, law enforcement has blamed the decentralization of central government powers for weakening police and encouraging civilians to take matters into their own hands. But "mob justice" is not a new phenomenon in Indonesia. It certainly did not begin with democratization.[71] These incidents can often be grisly and brutal, but they serve as a plaintive reminder that the Indonesian population is in need of a state that can protect its civilians, administer justice for wrongdoing, and resolve conflicts without bias or bribery. Supporting this conclusion, Barron, Kaiser, and Pradhan find that a local security presence – nearby security or police posts – coincides with lower levels of conflict.[72]

One of the main priorities of the early Reformasi period was getting the military out of the government. As early as November 1998, active military personnel were banned from holding civilian bureaucratic positions and the 75 military-designated seats in Parliament were cut to 38. In 2000, Parliament passed a decree obligating the military to give up all these seats by 2009.[73] Dwifungsi (dual-function), the Suharto-era doctrine that allowed the military to participate in ideological, political, economic, and socio-cultural matters (normally, beyond the military's purview) was eliminated, and the military was renamed from the Suharto-era ABRI (Angkatan Bersenjata Republik Indonesia) back to its original name, TNI (Tentara Nasional Indonesia).

At first, TNI insisted that only the military could initiate and propose military reform. But in 2000, Abdurrahman Wahid's then-Defence Minister, law professor Mahfud MD, rejected TNI's version of a new State Defence Bill, instead advising TNI to collaborate with the NGO ProPatria's Security Sector Reform Working Group and submit a joint-draft.[74] The final version included such stipulations as taking the responsibility for most internal security away from TNI and making it the sole purview of the now-independent national police, and making the civilian-led Ministry of Defence, not TNI, responsible for policy and strategy. In 2004, a similar activist-driven revamping altered the Armed Forces Bill. Most prominently, the Armed Forces Act required the government to take control of all military-owned businesses by 2009.[75] When push came to shove in 2009, however, a presidential decree was passed that allowed some military-owned businesses to be passed to military foundations or cooperatives.[76] Overall, the

Indonesian military has been placed under civilian command and is expected to adhere to international laws and human rights norms.

There is much room for improvement. A lingering culture of impunity, especially in cases of "revenge" for a brother-soldier's death, continues to exist within the ranks. Military justice was put under the control of the Supreme Court in 2005, but a 2008 attempt to subject military officers to civilian justice (including the police) for off-duty crimes has been stalled.[77] To some extent, the public continues to respect this culture although the newly-free press has not been shy to report stories about military wrongdoings.[78] At the same time, the court system has gradually become more likely to punish errant soldiers (see the 2013 Cebongan Prison Raid, for example). One glaring exception, galling to human rights activists, is the lack of legal action taken against military officers responsible for violence in Aceh, Papua, East Timor, or the May 1998 riots that forced Suharto from office. The popular assumption is that this immunity was the price to be paid for military acquiescence to civilian rule. In the spirit of forward progress and "reconciliation", it is highly unlikely that legal justice will be done in these cases.[79]

Since 2000, the exact execution of these new standards has depended in part on the President in power. Megawati Sukarnoputri was notably enthusiastic about using the military to reign in separatist movements in Aceh and Papua; on the other hand, Susilo Bambang Yudhoyono made military reform a priority, and has appointed like-minded military personnel, many trained in the 1980s with substantial portions of their careers taking place during the new era of Reformasi, to important TNI positions.

The two forms of violence that have attracted the most international attention and concern in post-Suharto Indonesia are separatism and terrorism. The August 1999 referendum that Habibie agreed to hold on East Timor's independence has been Indonesia's most radical shift towards decentralization to date. The East Timorese voted overwhelmingly to leave the Indonesian polity, triggering a violent response by the as-of-then unreformed TNI. This violence was witnessed by UN observers whom Habibie had expressly invited, and Indonesia was met with harsh international condemnation. The United States, for example, suspended its International Military Education and Training assistance programme for Indonesia. An Australia-led peacekeeping team took over, followed by the United Nations Transitional Administration in East Timor (UNTAET), until formal independence was finally obtained in 2002.

Letting a restive province choose to leave Indonesia was considered by some to be a tactical mistake on Habibie's part, even though it was clear that the status quo had become untenable in East Timor. The annexed territory had never been successfully assimilated into Indonesia; the Indonesian military treated the East Timorese with excessive brutality. One estimate received by the Commission for Reception, Truth and Reconciliation in East Timor estimates 102,800 conflict-related deaths (18,600 killings as well as indirect deaths from destitute conditions) in East Timor between 1974 and 1999.[80] The fact that the East Timorese voted so overwhelmingly for independence indicates that there was no other path forward. In October 1999, Indonesia repealed its annexation laws, and Habibie delivered an accountability speech that was rejected by Parliament, prompting him to withdraw his nomination to become Indonesia's next president.

Yet Habibie's successor, Abdurrahman Wahid, gave discontented provinces an even longer leash. He opened negotiations with the Free Aceh Movement (GAM) in March 2000, even suggesting an East Timor-style referendum in Aceh, and allowed West Papuans to raise the separatist Morning Star flag in September 2000. Megawati, who was very committed to the unchanging unity of the Indonesian polity, took a far more hardline approach to these provinces while still overseeing the signage of laws on special autonomy for both provinces. For the most part, Megawati managed to escape international criticism for her heavy-handed approach, in no small way because the threat of terrorism overtook concerns about human rights violations.

Indonesia expressed sympathy following 911, the attacks of 11 September 2011 by the Islamic terrorist group al-Queda on the United States, but was not entirely supportive of U.S. military action in Afghanistan. It also dismissed speculation that Southeast Asia might become the "second front" in the War on Terror, as well as concerns about the local terrorist network Jema'ah Islamiyah.[81] This changed after the Bali bombings on 12 October 2002, in which Jema'ah Islamiyah killed 202 people, including 164 foreigners. This attack shocked Indonesia into a decisive response: a successful counterterrorism campaign that had the support of moderate Muslim groups Muhammadiyah and Nahdlatul Ulama.

Despite some concerns about due process of law and state use of violence, the international community – and particularly the United States, which reinstated military support to assist in the counterterrorism effort – welcomed Indonesia's initiative. With the exception of two smaller attacks in Jakarta in August 2003 and September 2004, the threat of terrorism diminished in Indonesia.

Thanks to shrewd conciliatory policies offered by the Yudhoyono government, separatism is no longer an issue of great concern in Indonesia. Aceh is entitled to extra provisions of self-governance thanks to the Law of Governing Aceh (enacted in 2006 after the devastation of the 2004 tsunami and the setbacks suffered by GAM led to the 2005 Helsinki Peace Agreement), including representation by Aceh-only parties in Parliament, and the permission to implement sharia law. Many of Aceh's politicians are former GAM members, and the fact that the Indonesian Government has allowed them to hold office is indicative of the government's embrace of democratic principles. Papua was also granted measures of self-governance through Law 21/2001 on Special Autonomy in Papua. Compared to Aceh, the Indonesian government still has significant work to do in Papua. The special autonomy law has not always been faithfully implemented, Papua remains underdeveloped compared to the rest of Indonesia, and the Free Papua Movement (OPM) remains militant.[82] In a positive sign, Yudhoyono has explained that Indonesia is currently committed to resolving separatism through "peaceful resolutions" and "strongly factoring in local considerations".[83] Neither Aceh nor Papua have quite the autonomy that separatists would hope for, but the central government has made progress in winning their buy-in to the Indonesian nation-state.

A long-term concern about Indonesia's stability centres on the role of Islam. Indonesia is the world's largest Muslim country, with roughly 87 per cent of its population claiming adherence to a mostly moderate interpretation of the faith. Since independence, Islam has occupied a special role in the Indonesian polity. Historically, Indonesia's central government has opted to strike a balance between Islamists seeking to create a more openly theocratic state and secularists seeking to keep Islam out of the national foundation at all. This compromise has been achieved through an official emphasis on monotheism (rather than Islam per se) as a pillar of the Pancasila, the five principles of state, and careful control over Islamic groups. After all, militant Islamists have spearheaded failed rebellions in the past. During the Suharto era, the desire to control political Islam became excessive, with all Muslim parties being forced to merge into one big-tent party, the United Development Party (PPP). After the fall of Suharto, Islamic groups, like all other social forces in Indonesia, saw new room to stretch their legs. Some of these groups have been responsible for an increase in national instability. The Islamist militia Laskar Jihad's involvement in the Christian-Muslim conflict in Maluku, for example, led to a sharp escalation of violence there in 2000. These days, radical Islam takes on the form of moral vigilantism, epitomized by groups such as the Islamic Defenders Front (Front Pembela Islam, or FPI), which have attacked churchgoers, the minority, Muslim sect Ahmadiyah, and establishments that sell alcohol. But overall radical groups pose far less a challenge to Indonesia's stability than was feared by the international community a decade ago.

The fact that Indonesia has successfully consolidated its democracy, stabilized its economy, and achieved internal stability lends it a great deal of credibility within Southeast Asia and the region as a whole. The developing states of Southeast Asia have always placed a premium on economic growth and political stability – in the past, these two pursuits were associated with undemocratic authoritarian rule. While Indonesia was a regional leader under Suharto's rule it is only since his ouster that Indonesia has achieved the "holy trinity" – economic growth, internal stability, *and* an open democratic system, while re-emerging as a regional leader.

Meanwhile, Indonesia's attainment of the trifecta of democracy, economic growth, and stability has also boosted its weight in multilateral organizations such as the G-20. Under President Yudhoyono, Indonesia has started to embrace its role as a "success story" as well as rediscovered the possibility of serving as a voice for developing countries. As former Trade Minister Mari Pangestu explained: "[Indonesia's] experience is one that we would like to be able to share with the rest of the world."[84]

Notes

[1] This chapter is co-authored with Nadia Bulkin.

[2] President Susilo Bambang Yudhoyono, conversation with the author, Jakarta, 16 January 2014.

[3] Ibid.

[4]   Ibid.

[5]   Donald Horowitz, *Constitutional Change and Democracy in Indonesia*, (Cambridge, UK: Cambridge University Press, 2013), p. 93.

[6]   "Voter turnout data for Indonesia", Institute for Democracy and Electoral Assistance, 5 October 2011 <http://www.idea.int/vt/countryview. cfm?CountryCode=ID>

[7]   Andrew Thornley, "Nine Takeaways from Indonesia's Legislative Elections", *The Asia Foundation*, 16 April 2014 <http://asiafoundation.org/in-asia/2014/04/16/ nine-takeaways-from-indonesias-legislative-elections/>

[8]   Jamie S. Davidson, "Dilemmas of democratic consolidation in Indonesia", *The Pacific Review* 22, no. 3 (2009): 293–310.

[9]   Greg Fealy, "Political Islam on the rebound in Indonesia", *Brisbane Times*, 15 April 2014 <http://www.brisbanetimes.com.au/comment/political-islam-on-the- rebound-in-indonesia-20140415-zqv1e.html>

[10] Greg Fealy, "Resurgent political Islam, or astute Islamic parties?" *New Mandala*, 14 April 2014 <http://asiapacific.anu.edu.au/newmandala/2014/04/14/resurgent- political-islam-or-astute-islamic-parties/>

[11] Horowitz, op. cit, p. 72.

[12] Joshua Kurlantzick, "Indonesia: Political and Economic Lessons From Democ- ratic Transitions", Council on Foreign Relations, 2013 <http://www.cfr.org/ democratization/indonesia/p30816>

[13] Damien Kingsbury, *The Politics of Indonesia*, 3rd edition (Oxford, UK: Oxford University Press, 2005).

[14] Sulfikar Amir, "Nuclear revival in post-Suharto Indonesia", *Asian Survey* 50, no. 2 (2010): 281–82.

[15] Davidson, op. cit., p. 294.

[16] Greg Fealy, "Indonesian Politics in 2011: Democratic Regression and Yudhoyono's Regal Incumbency", *Bulletin of Indonesian Economic Studies* 47, no. 3 (2011): 349.

[17] Lex Rieffel, "Indonesia's Quiet Revolution", *Foreign Affairs* 83, no. 5 (2004): 109.

[18] Marcus Mietzner, "Indonesia's Democratic Stagnation: Anti-Reformist Elites and Resilient Civil Society", *Democratizaton* 19, no. 2 (2012): 209–29.

[19] Kurlantzick, op. cit.

[20] "Remarks by the President at the University of Indonesia in Jakarta, Indonesia", The White House Office of the Press Secretary, 10 November 2010 <http:// www.whitehouse.gov/the-press-office/2010/11/10/remarks-president-university- indonesia-jakarta-indonesia>

[21] Larry Diamond, "How is Indonesia's democracy doing?" *East Asia Forum*, 26 October 2009 <http://www.eastasiaforum.org/2009/10/26/how-is-indonesias- democracy-doing/>

[22] Horowitz, op. cit.

23   Phillips Vermonte, interview with the author, Jakarta, 12 March 2014.

24   The data for his observation was taken from a doctoral thesis at the Department of Political Science, Gadjah Mada University, Yogyakarta, by Idrus Marham, the secretary of Golkar's faction in the Parliament and Vice-Chairman of Commission II; Ignas Kleden, "Democracy ... its constraints", *Jakarta Post*, 25 January 2009 <http://www.thejakartapost.com/news/2009/01/25/democracy-its-constraints.html>

25   Kurlantzick, op. cit.

26   Mietzner, op. cit., p. 215.

27   Robert Klitgaard, Ronald MacLean-Abaroa and H. Lindsey Parris, "A Practical Approach to Dealing with Municipal Malfeasance", Urban Management Programme Working Paper Series No. 7, (Nairobi, 1996) pp. 10–11.

28   Baladas Ghoshal, "In Myanmar's transition, shades of Indonesia", *The Hindu*, 9 January 2013 <http://www.thehindu.com/opinion/op-ed/in-myanmars-transition-shades-of-indonesia/article4287613.ece>

29   "Indonesia GDP Annual Growth Rate", *Trading Economics* <http://www.tradingeconomics.com/indonesia/gdp-growth-annual> (accessed 20 January 2014)

30   *Asian Development Outlook 2013 Update*. (Manila: ADB, 2013)<http://www.adb.org/countries/indonesia/economy> (accessed on 22 January 2014)

31   Raoul Oberman, Richard Dobbs, Arief Budiman, Fraser Thompson, and Morten Rossé, "The archipelago economy: Unleashing Indonesia's potential", *McKinsey Global Institute*, September 2012, pp. 1,3.

32   Didi Kirsten Tatlow, "BRIC, BRICS or BRICSI? The Growing Challenge", *New York Times*, 28 March 2013 <http://rendezvous.blogs.nytimes.com/2013/03/28/first-bric-then-brics-now-bricsi-the-world-financial-orders-challenge/?_php=true&_type=blogs&_r=0> (accessed 21 January 2014)

33   "Asian Financial Crisis in Indonesia", *Indonesia Investments* <http://www.indonesia-investments.com/culture/economy/asian-financial-crisis/item246> (accessed 2 May 2014)

34   "Indonesia Overview", The World Bank <http://www.worldbank.org/en/country/indonesia/overview> (accessed on 22 January 2014)

35   Oberman et al., op. cit.; Martin Hahn, "Indonesia Outperforms Goldman Sachs' BRIC Countries", 3 November 2012. <http://ivn.us/2012/11/03/indonesia-outperforms-goldman-sachs-bric-countries/> (accessed on 21 January 2014)

36   Rieffel, op. cit., p. 107.

37   Tatlow, op. cit.

38   Suresh P. Singh and Memory Dube, "BRICS and the World Order: A Beginner's Guide", February 2013 Global Economic Governance – Africa (GEGAfrica) and South African Institute of International Affairs <http://cuts-international.org/BRICS-TERN/pdf/BRICS_and_the_World_Order-A_Beginners_Guide.pdf> (Accessed on 2 May 2014)

39 Karen Brooks, "Is Indonesia Bound for the BRICs? How Stalling Reform Could Hold Jakarta Back", *Foreign Affairs*, November/December 2011 <http://www.foreignaffairs.com/articles/136539/karen-brooks/is-indonesia-bound-for-the-brics> (accessed on 21 January 2014)

40 Alison Hall, "BRIC Is Now BRIICS for Global Companies", Global Intelligence Alliance, 1 August 2012 <http://meetingsnet.com/global-site-research/bric-now-briics-global-companies> (accessed on 22 January 2014)

41 Maureen Farrell, "Indonesia: The newest BRIC?" *CNN Money Invest*, 24 October 2012 <http://money.cnn.com/2012/10/15/investing/indonesia-bric/> (accessed on 21 January 2014)

42 Oberman et al., op. cit., p. 4.

43 Ibid., p. 1.

44 Marcus Mietzner, "Fighting the Hellhounds: Pro-democracy Activists and Party Politics in Post-Suherto Indonesia", *Journal of Contemporary Asia* 43, no.1 (2013).

45 "Indonesia Overview", op. cit.

46 Oberman et al., op. cit., p. 8.

47 Ibid, p. 3.

48 Ibid, p. 7.

49 "Logistics Performance Index", The World Bank, 2014. <http://lpi.worldbank.org/international/global> (accessed on 5 May 2014)

50 Janeman Latul and Neil Chatterjee, "Special report: The missing BRIC in Indonesia's wall", 19 January 2012 <http://www.reuters.com/article/2012/01/19/us-indonesia-infrastructure-idUSTRE80I0HH20120119> (accessed on 22 January 2014)

51 Kurlantzick, op. cit.

52 "Indonesia in Focus: Election special", Berwin Leighton Paisner, April 2014 <http://www.blplaw.com/download/IFG_Apr2014.pdf>

53 Thee Kian Wie, "Understanding Indonesia: The Role of Economic Nationalism", *Journal of Indonesian Social Sciences and Humanities* 3(2010): 77.

54 Rieffel, op. cit., p. 108.

55 Soemadipradja, Rahmat, and Matthew Goerke, "The 2009 Mining Law Justifiable protection of national sovereignty, or damaging resource nationalism?" *Engineering and Mining Journal* 213, no. 7 (2012): 70.

56 "Indonesia to ease export tax, 1st rollback of mining rules", *Reuters*, 24 February 2014. <http://www.reuters.com/article/2014/02/24/indonesia-minerals-idUSL3N0LT1V620140224>

57 "Economic Outlook, Bilateral Trade & Investment Opportunities with Indonesia", Presentation by Indonesia's Commercial Attaché to the U.S., Annapolis International Club, 6 November 2013.

58 Ashutosh Varshney, Rizal Panggabean, and Mohammad Zulfan Tadjoeddin, "Patterns of Collective Violence in Indonesia (1990–2003)", United Nations Support Facility for Indonesian Recovery (UNSFIR) Working Paper 04/03 (2004)

p. 30. <http://www.conflictrecovery.org/bin/Patterns_of_collective_violence_July04.pdf>

59   "Indonesia: The Violence in Ambon", Human Rights Watch, March 1999 <http://www.hrw.org/legacy/reports/1999/ambon/>

60   Lorraine V. Aragon, "Waiting for peace in Poso." *Inside Indonesia* vol. 70 (April-June 2002) <http://www.insideindonesia.org/feature-editions/waiting-for-peace-in-poso>

61   Jim Della-Giacoma, "What could Myanmar learn from Indonesia: The Malino Accord", International Crisis Group, 4 September 2012. <http://www.crisisgroupblogs.org/resolvingconflict/2012/09/04/what-could-myanmar-learn-from-indonesia-the-malino-accord/>

62   Smith Alhadar, "The forgotten war in North Maluku", *Inside Indonesia*, vol. 63 (July-September 2000) <http://www.insideindonesia.org/weekly-articles/the-forgotten-war-in-north-maluku>

63   "Indonesia: The Moluccas agreement in Malino (Malino II) signed to end conflict and create peace in the Moluccas", Government of Indonesia, 14 February 2002. <http://reliefweb.int/report/indonesia/indonesia-moluccas-agreement-malino-malino-ii-signed-end-conflict-and-create-peace>

64   Michael Vatikiotis, "Resolving conflict in Indonesia", *Jakarta Post*, 30 July 2011 <http://www.thejakartapost.com/news/2011/07/30/resolving-conflict-indonesia.html>

65   "Conflict Management Strategies in Indonesia: Learning from the Maluku Experience", Workshop Report, Centre for Humanitarian Dialogue, 2010. <http://www.hdcentre.org/uploads/tx_news/21ConflictManagementStrategiesinMaluku01032010_0.pdf>

66   Chris Wilson, "Internal Conflict in Indonesia: Causes, Symptoms and Sustainable Resolution", Research Paper 1 2001–02, Foreign Affairs, Defence and Trade Group, Parliament of Australia, 7 August 2001. <http://www.aph.gov.au/About_Parliament/Parliamentary_Departments/Parliamentary_Library/pubs/rp/rp0102/02RP01#section1>

67   Varshney, Panggabean, and Tadjoeddin, op. cit., pp. 24–25.

68   Ibid, p. 23.

69   Aceh, Maluku, Maluku Utara, Papua, Papua Barat, Kalimantan Barat, NTT, Sulawesi Tengah, Kalimantan Tengah. While the data, especially exact numbers of conflicts, casualties and damages, cannot be entirely precise, it does confirm the general impression of lessening intensity of violence in Indonesia.

70   Patrick Barron, Kai Kaiser, and Menno Pradhan, "Local Conflict in Indonesia: Measuring Incidence and Identifying Patterns", World Bank Policy Research Working Papers, August 2004 pp. 31–32.

71   Varshney, Panggabean, and Tadjoeddin, op. cit., p. 17.

72   Barron, Kaiser, and Pradhan, op. cit., p. 32.

73   Brian Vogt, "The Path to Civilian Rule in Burma Goes Through Indonesia", Center for National Policy, February 2014, p. 4. <http://cnponline.org/wp-content/

uploads/2014/04/The-Path-to-Civilian-Rule-in-Burma-Goes-through-Indonesia. pdf>

74   Mietzner (2013), op. cit., p. 34–35.

75   Mietzner (2013), op. cit., p. 36; Davidson, op. cit., p. 294.

76   Vogt, op. cit., p. 4.

77   Horowitz, op. cit., p. 218.

78   Vogt, op. cit., p. 5.

79   Kurlantzick, op. cit.

80   Romesh Silva and Patrick Ball, "A Report by the Benetech Human Rights Data Analysis Group to the Commission on Reception, Truth and Reconciliation of Timor-Leste", Benetech. 9 February 2006 <https://hrdag.org/content/timorleste/ Benetech-Report-to-CAVR.pdf>

81   Mark Manyin, "*Terrorism in Southeast Asia*", Congressional Research Service Report for Congress, 18 November 2003 <http://www.history.navy.mil/library/online/ terrorism%20in%20southeast%20asia.htm>

82   Jason MacLeod, "Movements and Campaigns", Written in August 2009 and updated in March 2011 <http://www.nonviolent-conflict.org/index.php/ movements-and-campaigns/movements-and-campaigns-summaries?sobi2Id=1&s obi2Task=sobi2Details>

83   Susilo Bambang Yudhoyono, Keynote Speech for the Special Plenary of the 36th Session of the General Conference in Celebration of the 10th Anniversary of the UNESCO Universal Declaration on Cultural Diversity <http://www.unesco.org/ eri/publications/36GC/Decl_cult_div_speeches_indonesia.pdf>

84   "A new boss for the World Trade Organisation", interview with Mari Elka Pangestu, *Australia Network*, 12 February 2013. <http://www.abc.net.au/ australianetwork/focus/s3692612.htm>

Chapter 3

INDONESIA AND
THE REGIONAL ARCHITECTURE

A key aspect of Indonesia's foreign policy, one that separates Indonesia from the BRICS and many of G-20 members, is to use regional legitimacy as the foundation for global status. Such a policy, termed as a "regionalist approach to globalism", reflects two realities. The first is that in terms of material power, Indonesia is mainly a regional power. The second is that ideationally, Indonesia has conceived of a foreign policy role that puts a premium on regional order as the basis of its global role. Hence, Indonesia's approach sees its foreign policy and external role in terms of a series of "concentric circles".

> The first concentric circle is with Association of Southeast Asian Nations (ASEAN) which becomes Indonesia's prime pillar in carrying out its foreign policies. In the second concentric circle lies ASEAN + 3 (Japan, China, South Korea). Outside of those circles, Indonesia also builds an intensive cooperation with the USA and European Union which serve as Indonesia's main economic partners. In the third concentric circle lie like-minded developing countries.[1]

ASEAN

Within the concentric circles approach, ASEAN has been the cornerstone of Indonesia's foreign policy. Indonesia's turn to regional cooperation predates ASEAN or dates back to the earliest years of the republic. In Indonesia one finds a striking case of how nationalism and regionalism can converge, or how regionalism can be turned into a tool of national liberation. Thus, the cause of Indonesia's independence was strongly championed by a group of its neighbours who, led by India, organized the Conference on Indonesia in New Delhi in

1949 to protest against the vestiges of Dutch colonialism and its "police action" in the country, which had already declared its independence in 1947. It was Indonesia which proposed the conference of Asian and African nations which was held in Bandung during 18–24 April 1955. In 2005, Indonesia hosted the 50th anniversary of that conference, which had not only laid the foundation of the Non-Aligned Movement, but also had an enduring impact in shaping the contours of Indonesia's foreign policy.

But Indonesia's founding President Sukarno's ambitions extended beyond what is today known as Southeast Asia. To be sure, the idea of Southeast Asia as a distinctive region was itself very new and right up until after the Bandung conference, countries that are today seen as part of "South Asia" such as India, Pakistan and Ceylon were regarded as Southeast Asian nations. Indonesia was not part of the Association of Southeast Asia (ASA), formed in 1961 by Thailand, Malaysia and the Philippines, although it floundered over the Philippines' claim to Sabah, which had opted to join the Malaysian Federation. Indonesia's relations with its immediate neighbours turned rocky when Sukarno launched its policy of Konfrontasi against Malaysia in 1963. That move doomed the idea of MAPHILINDO, anacronym for a loose confederation of three independent states of Malaya stock (Indonesia, Malaya and the Philippines), which had been proposed in 1963.

The end of Konfrontasi and the regime change from Sukarno to Suharto (the two events were not unrelated) led to a major shift in Indonesia's interest and involvement in Southeast Asian regionalism, which found its most concrete expression in the establishment of the Association of Southeast Asian Nations (ASEAN) in 1967. Indonesia's position in ASEAN has been described variously as being that of *primus inter pares* (first among the equals) and likened to being a "hostage" or being in a "golden cage". A decade and half later, a noted Indonesian strategic analyst, J. Soedjati Djiwandono, would describe Indonesia's golden cage in the following words:

> Indonesia's membership within ASEAN would reduce the possibility of threat to their security posed by their giant neighbor…Indonesia would appear to be placed in what amounts to a 'hostage' position, albeit in a golden cage. For the new leadership in Jakarta…it is within ASEAN that Indonesia might be provided with an opportunity to realize its ambitions, if any, to occupy a position of primacy or primus inter pares without recourse to a policy of confrontation.[2]

In supporting ASEAN, Suharto's New Order was pursuing both a foreign policy philosophy as well as immediate considerations of regime security and international legitimacy. In her seminal book on Indonesia's role in ASEAN, Dewi Fortuna Anwar argues that:

> The New Order leaders saw several benefits in Indonesia actively participating in regional co-operation immediately in the wake of confrontation. Uppermost in their minds was the urgent need to restore Indonesia's credibility both in the region and in the wider international community, especially in the West. Indonesia had to refurbish its image abroad and convince the West that the new government was really worth supporting.[3]

But ASEAN also upheld Indonesia's idea of an "independent and active" foreign policy. It was consistent with Indonesia's refusal in 1954 to join SEATO, despite an invitation from the UK (acting on behalf of the Eisenhower administration) and its determination to seek "regional solutions to regional problems". At the founding Bangkok meeting in August 1967, Indonesia expressed the view, as summarized in a confidential British diplomatic memo, that "Indonesia always wanted to see South East Asia develop into a region which could stand on its own feet, strong enough to defend itself against any negative influences from outside the region".[4] Whereas SEATO was seen by Indonesia as an instrument of the Cold War which made Southeast Asian countries dependent on outside powers for their security and development. ASEAN would represent an indigenous approach to regional security and development. In a 1970 essay, Indonesian Foreign Minister Adam Malik drew attention to the danger of participating in great power military alliances or hosting foreign military bases when he warned that "military alliances or foreign military presence does not enhance a nation's capacity to cope with the problem of insurgency. The price for such commitments is too high, whereas the negative ramifications for the nation are too great."[5] Later, he would highlight the benefit of regional cooperation, which would allow ASEAN countries to make a bigger impact on international affairs than if they acted individually:

> Southeast Asia is one region in which the presence and interests of most major powers converge, politically as well as physically. The frequency and intensity

of policy interactions among them, as well as their dominant influence on the countries in the region, cannot but have a direct bearing on political realities. In the face of this, the smaller nations of the region have no hope of ever making any impact on this pattern of dominant influence of the big powers, unless they act collectively and until they develop the capacity to forge among themselves an area of internal cohesion, stability and common purpose. Thus regional cooperation within ASEAN also came to represent the conscious effort by its member countries to try to re-assert their position and contribute their own concepts and goals within the ongoing process of stabilization of a new power equilibrium in the region.[6]

It was through ASEAN that Indonesia was able to "export" or multilateralize its "independent and active" foreign policy doctrine by developing a 'regional solutions to regional problems' position. To quote Malik again:

> Regional problems, i.e. those having a direct bearing upon the region concerned, should be accepted as being of primary concern to that region itself. Mutual consultations and cooperation among the countries of the region in facing these problems may…lead to the point where the views of the region are accorded the primacy they deserve in these arch for solution.[7]

Indonesia rejected not only the SEATO model of a superpower-led military alliance, but also any regional organisation dominated or likely to be dominated by a major Asian or Western power, such as the Asia-Pacific Council (proposed by South Korea in 1964, and including among its members Japan and Australia). At the same time, Indonesia saw ASEAN as a forum with which to manage intra-regional disputes by providing its good offices and mediation role. An early and prime example of this role was Indonesia's mediation in dispute between Malaysia and the Philippines over Sabah in the late 1960s. After the dispute had paralysed the fledgling ASEAN, Indonesia played an active role in 1968 and 1969 in persuading the two sides to agree to a "cooling-off period", which subsequently paved the way for the conflict to be "swept under the carpet", if not permanently resolved.[8] The other major manifestation of Indonesia's regional mediation role was the decade-long Cambodia conflict triggered by the Vietnamese invasion of Cambodia in December 1978. While Indonesia condemned the Vietnamese invasion, its approach to the conflict differed from the policy of the US and China. While the US and China sought to punish

Indonesia's first President Sukarno arriving at the venue of the Asia-Africa Conference in Bandung on 18 April 1955. The Conference, which was a precursor to the Non-Aligned Movement, was a symbol of Indonesia's "independent and active" foreign policy and its leadership aspirations in the developing world.

Indonesia's first directly elected President, Susilo Bambang Yudhoyono at a dinner with fellow ASEAN leaders at the 22nd ASEAN Summit in 2013 in Brunei. After a period of uncertainty following the ouster of Suharto in 1998, Indonesia resumed a leadership role in ASEAN. ASEAN leadership is a key basis of Indonesia's role as a regional power with global interests and concerns. (Source: Photo by Cahyo/presidenri.go.id)

President Yudhoyono responding to journalists in front of United Nations Headquarters in New York. Next to him is Foreign Minister (since 2009) Marty Natalegawa, who has championed the idea of "dynamic equilibrium" in Indonesia's approach to security in the Asia-Pacific and Indo-Pacific regions. (*Source*: Photo by muchlis/presidenri.go.id)

President Yudhoyono with German Chancellor Angela Merkel and US President Barack Obama at the G-20 Summit in St Petersburg in 2013. Membership in the G-20 grouping, which played a vital role in managing the 2008 global financial crisis, has allowed Indonesia to project an active profile on the global stage. (*Source*: Photo by anung/presidenri.go.id)

Hassan Wirajuda, Indonesia's Foreign Minister 2001–09, who made democracy promotion a key element of Indonesia's foreign policy under the democratic system.

The author with Major General Bachtiar (commander of Kodam VII/Wirabuana) and his staff in Makassar, South Sulawesi. Civilian control of the military and security sector reform has been a key basis of Indonesia's democratic transition.

Indonesian Defence Minister Purnomo Yusgiantoro discussing Indonesian defence policy, with the author in Jakarta in January 2014.

Posters for the legislative elections in Manado, North Sulawesi, March 2014. A vibrant democracy including free and fair elections has helped Indonesia to gain international respect and pursue its regional and global leadership aspirations.

The author addressing students at Pondok Pesantren, An-Nahdlah, Makasar. (*Source*: Anak Agung Ngurah Andy Laksmana)

The Indonesian Election Commission's official poster listing the candidates for the presidency and vice-presidency in the 2014 presidential elections. (*Source*: I Sade Bimanatara)

and "bleed" Vietnam by arming the coalition of forces resisting Vietnamese occupation and the US used Cambodia as a test of the Reagan Doctrine of "rolling back" Soviet gains in the Third World, Indonesia, while remaining firmly opposed to the Vietnamese occupation of Cambodia, led the ASEAN effort to find a diplomatic solution to the conflict. Jakarta believed that a prolonged stalemate in the conflict was harming ASEAN and regional stability by aggravating the Cold War great power rivalry in Southeast Asia. Indonesia's effort was spearheaded first by Mochtar Kusumaatmadja (Foreign Minister 1978–88), and then by Ali Alatas (Foreign Minister 1988–99). Indonesia-sponsored "proximity talks", and "cocktail diplomacy", followed by successive Jakarta informal meetings in July 1988 and February 1989 that laid the groundwork for the Paris Peace Conferences on Cambodia in 1989and 1991 that resulted in the settlement of the Cambodia conflict.

After the Cambodia settlement, Indonesia continued to play a key role in ASEAN. However, its leadership was rarely overbearing; nor would it deny leadership to other members in specific issue areas. It could be said that ASEAN has no single leader. At various stages, Thailand (which introduced the idea of "flexible engagement" or moving away from strict non-interference in ASEAN), Malaysia (which proposed the idea of East Asian Economic Caucus/Grouping), Singapore (on the ASEAN Free Trade Area) and the Philippines (on the ASEAN socio-cultural community) have played instrumental roles shaping ASEAN's position and agenda.

The fall of Suharto in 1998 raised questions about Indonesia's commitment to ASEAN. Not only did ASEAN lose a staunch supporter in Suharto, but some analysts and neighbouring countries wondered if Indonesia might return to Sukarno era nationalism at the expense of regionalism. Under the Jusuf Habibie and Abdurrahman Wahid governments, Indonesia's foreign policy seemed to lack focus and drive, especially when it came to leading ASEAN.[9] While Indonesia under President Megawati Sukarnoputri did initiate the ASEAN Security Community idea; it was however mainly an initiative of the Foreign Ministry. Preoccupation with domestic issues and the process of democratic consolidation constrained post-Suharto Indonesia's ability to have an active foreign policy, and claim its leadership role in ASEAN.

One of the major turnarounds in Indonesian foreign policy after Suharto occurred when Susilo Bambang Yudhoyono took office as the first directly elected

President of the country. Among his first tasks was to return Indonesia to the centre-stage of regional cooperation initiatives, especially ASEAN. Yudhoyono, who is described by some of his associates as the most activist president in foreign policy domain since Sukarno, would tell his fellow ASEAN leaders that "Indonesia is back".[10] Not only was Indonesia reengaged in ASEAN, it also sought to reform the organization. Taking lessons from ASEAN's meek response to the 1997 Asian financial crisis, it led efforts to develop a more open ASEAN which would move away from its strict non-interference doctrine. As part of this effort, it pushed for the realization of an ASEAN Security Community (ASC, later renamed as the ASEAN Political-Security Community, although here I will continue to use the ASC) and championed human rights and democracy in ASEAN, including political reform in Myanmar and the creation of an ASEAN human rights mechanism.

The ASC was the most important example of the new Indonesia's regional role. Formally proposed by Indonesia in 2003, just before it assumed the rotating chair of the ASEAN Standing Committee (July 2003–July 2004),[11] the ASC was aimed at reviving ASEAN whose credibility had suffered since the 1997 economic crisis. Some of the motivations behind the Indonesian initiative included concerns over Singapore–Malaysia tensions, the need to dilute the non-intervention principle (non-intervention had made it difficult for deeper cooperation on internal matters with regional or transnational impact), and the need for a security pillar for ASEAN to complement the Singapore-proposed ASEAN Economic Community (could these not be an economic community without a political-security foundation?)[12]

Indonesia's interest in deepening ASEAN cooperation through the ASC idea was also influenced by the rising threat posed by non-traditional security issues, such as the terrorist bombing in Bali in 2002 and in the Jakarta Marriott Hotel bombing in 2003, the Severe Acute Respiratory Syndrome (SARS) crisis in 2003, the tsunami triggered by an earthquake off the west coast of Sumatra on 26 December 2004. The tsunami led to at least 128,000 deaths and 37,000 missing. Another such challenge has been the haze from forest fires in Sumatra and Kalimantan, which, as will be discussed later in this chapter, has caused much controversy in the region and put Indonesia in a negative light.

According to the Indonesian thinking at this time, the ASC concept would be based on "a fundamental, unambiguous and long-term convergence of interests among ASEAN members in the avoidance of war".[13] It also called for norm setting with outside (extra regional) powers through measures such as extending the scope for their accession to the ASEAN Treaty of Amity and Cooperation (TAC), as well as through the development of a code of conduct in the South China Sea between ASEAN and China. The Indonesian proposal contained several measures to advance political and security cooperation in ASEAN including meetings among an ASEAN Defence and Home Ministers, and creation of new mechanisms for cooperation on non-traditional security issues, such as terrorism, a regional peacekeeping force and initiatives for resolving conflicts among members including negotiations and facilitation/ mediation by the ASEAN High Council. Other proposed measures would promote "political development" within the ASC through democracy, an ASEAN Human Rights Commission, and good governance. Subsequently, some of these proposals would be dropped due to resistance from the more conservative ASEAN members. But what was clear was that Indonesia was placing ASEAN on an entirely new footing, with a more open and liberal outlook. It had shed its earlier reservations about diluting non-interference (in 1998, Ali Alatas had managed to rename then Thai Foreign Minister Surin Pitsuwan's idea of "flexible engagement" to a more conservative notion of "enhanced interaction").

The ASC concept was formally adopted as ASEAN Political and Security Community at ASEAN's Bali Summit in October 2003. Some in ASEAN saw Indonesia's role in this as a bid to reassert itself over the rest of the region. But Indonesian policymakers like Hassan Wirajuda firmly dismissed this criticism. For him the ASC was never intended to be a "projection of Indonesian hegemonic power".[14] Another challenge to Indonesia's leadership comes from within Indonesia. For example a leading analyst like Rizal Sukma has advocated a "post-ASEAN foreign policy" for Indonesia. Sukma argues that Indonesia should not limit itself to viewing ASEAN as the cornerstone of Indonesia's foreign policy.[15]

> Indonesia...needs to begin formulating a post-ASEAN foreign policy. ASEAN should no longer be treated as the only cornerstone of Indonesia's foreign policy. For Indonesia, ASEAN should constitute only one of the available platforms

through which we can attain and fulfill our national interests. Some of our foreign policy initiatives – such as the Bali Democracy Forum (BDF), the G20 and strategic partnerships with global and regional major powers – have already shown signs toward that direction.[16]

Sukma's rationale for a post-ASEAN Indonesian role reflects exasperation with Indonesia's recent bilateral problems, especially the dispute with Malaysia over the Ambalat maritime area in the Celebes Sea, where Indonesia feels its sovereignty was being violated by Malaysian naval deployments. (The area was not covered by the ruling of the 2002 International Court of Justice which settled the Indonesia-Malaysia dispute over the Sipadan and Ligitan islands that ruled in Malaysia's favour). The sense here is why should Indonesia continue to exercise restraint towards its neighbours for the sake of ASEAN when they are not respectful of Indonesia's core interests. Sukma also argues that Indonesia should not sacrifice its democratic values for the sake of the authoritarian countries in ASEAN, for example defending Myanmar (before its recent democratic opening) in international fora.[17] Sukma does not, however, call for totally ignoring ASEAN. "For Indonesia, ASEAN should continue to be an important forum for managing inter-state relations among Southeast Asian countries through peaceful means."[18] But it should pay more attention to the wider regional context. He does not believe that Indonesia can play a truly global role, given the constraints on its power projection and the complexity of its domestic politics management. But it can play a more dynamic and assertive role in the wider Asia-Pacific and Indo-Pacific regions. Strategic developments especially the rise of China and the US "rebalancing" policy requires that Indonesia pays more attention to the changing strategic equation in this wider theatre rather than limiting itself to Southeast Asia per se.[19]

Sukma's advocacy of a "post-ASEAN foreign policy" is questioned by others. Challenging the perception that Indonesia has "outgrown" ASEAN already, Dewi Fortuna Anwar counters that it is the cornerstone of the country's foreign policy mainly because of the belief in the power of "ASEAN centrality" to shape East Asian regional architecture. Nonetheless, while ASEAN remains "indispensable for managing relations with major powers, Indonesian policy makers believe that the bloc should be ambitious about spreading its code of conduct, and that it should drive initiatives for creating a regional architecture in East Asia".[20]

Many Indonesians believe that Indonesia holds the key to ASEAN's future, as exemplified by the following comments by an Indonesian graduate student in Australia. He argues that while the "future of ASEAN…not only depend on the 'Indonesia' factor, but also on how the idea of regionalism embedded in the region and to the extent ASEAN countries' ability to overcome domestic impediments", Indonesia will be a central force deciding ASEAN's future. The "'Indonesia' factor…indeed has a big influence in determining the future of ASEAN. If Indonesia is keeping its leadership pace towards the future then it is likely the APSC [ASEAN Political-Security Community] will be strengthened and become a more integrated political security community that has a permanent dispute settlement mechanism. In sum, the role Indonesia seeks to play in ASEAN will determine the future of ASEAN."(sic)[21]

Indonesia continues to be active in its diplomacy of mediation and reconciliation in ASEAN. Two recent efforts attest to this. The first was its playing a good offices role in the escalating Preah Vihear dispute between Cambodia and Thailand in 2011, a situation that Foreign Minister Natalegawa described as having the potential to make "ASEAN a laughing stock" and risked "the collapse of the whole ASEAN enterprise".[22] Although his diplomacy including travels to both capitals did not settle the dispute (it was not expected to), which was referred to the International Court of Justice, it created a "sigh of relief" in ASEAN.[23] It did serve to ease tensions by raising before the two parties the collective concern of ASEAN.[24]

A second episode took placed in July 2013, when Natalegawa undertook a two-day shuttle diplomacy around Southeast Asia after ASEAN Foreign Ministers had embarrassingly failed to issue a joint communique at the end of their annual ministerial meeting in Cambodia held during 9–13 July. The failure to issue the communique, which Natalegawa would later describe as "one of the lowest points of my diplomatic career"[25] was over disagreements between the refusal of the ASEAN Chair Cambodia, taking a pro-China stance, to incorporate the positions of the Philippines and Vietnam regarding their territorial dispute with China in the South China Sea. The Indonesian effort led to a consensus on six principles on the South China Sea.[26]

In addition to this is Indonesia's ongoing mediation between the Philippine Government and the Moro National Liberation Front (MNLF) in seeking a solution to the insurgency in Mindanao, Philippines. Moreover, in April 2013, ASEAN launched an Indonesian initiative, the ASEAN Institute of Peace and Reconciliation (AIPR), whose goal is to promote peaceful approaches to domestic and inter-state conflicts by drawing, implicitly from Indonesia's recent successes in these areas (such as Aceh).

Indonesian leaders are especially proud of their role in championing human rights and democracy in ASEAN. According to Natalegawa, Indonesia made democracy and human rights, "part of the ASEAN lexicon".[27] Wirajuda stresses that the push to establish the ASEAN Intergovernmental Commission on Human Rights (AIHCR), established in 2009, was an "Indonesian initiative", although the idea of such a mechanism goes back to the early 1990s and it was mentioned in the ASEAN Charter adopted in 2008. As he put it, "other regional organizations were discussing human rights and democracy, but not ASEAN. How can ASEAN be successful if it is allergic to human rights and democracy?"[28] Initially the idea of such a mechanism faced resistance from other ASEAN countries on the ground of "Asian values". He opposed the concept of Asian values: "what Asian values, these are authoritarian values". There was "quite a battle" within ASEAN over this. While the AICHR exists, it has been criticized for lacking teeth. Its mandate is the "promotion" rather than the "protection" of human rights, which would require authority to conduct investigations and impose sanctions in the case of non-compliance. Wirajuda agrees with its critics that without authority for the protection mandate the AICHR is "inferior to international or Indonesian national commission's standard".[29] But the Declaration has its defenders, even among the civil society groups. As Rafendi Djamin, the Indonesian member of the AICHR argues, the document is by necessity a consensus text, the outcome of political negotiation among different political systems. The Declaration while not legally-binding, is nonetheless a "living document", and "the beginning, not the end" of a process of promoting human rights in the region. Among other things, it will help inspire a sense of ownership among ASEAN members on human rights. Thus, it is "not a perfect declaration but not a disaster".[30]

While reaffirming ASEAN's importance to Indonesia's foreign policy, Jakarta has also extended its efforts to maintain stability and security to the wider region. A notable initiative, as noted in Chapter 1, is its proposal for an Indo-Pacific Treaty of Friendship and Cooperation, which is to be founded upon the twelve Bali Principles adopted at the 2011 East Asian Summit in Bali (to be discussed shortly). And Foreign Minister Marty Natalegawa speaks of Indonesia's vision to move ASEAN as a collective force in the global arena: an "ASEAN Community in A Global Community of Nations".[31] The aim of this is to "make ASEAN speak on global issues", since Indonesia believes ASEAN is "punching below our weight" and can do more.[32] A Thai journalist, Kavi Chongkittavorn, observes that Indonesia is seeking to expand ASEAN's role beyond Southeast Asia. "Indonesia, as the only ASEAN member of the G-20, prefers that ASEAN moves beyond its passive and narrow geographical narratives to incorporate a broader global perspective."[33] Indeed, in his speech at the Opening Ceremony of the 19th ASEAN Summit on November 2011, President Yudhoyono underscored the need not only to strengthen the three pillars of the ASEAN Community (economic, political-security and socio-cultural), but also the importance of ASEAN taking "on a leading role in designing a more efficient and effective architecture regional cooperation", and "strengthen the role of ASEAN globally".[34]

Indonesia is not without bilateral disputes with its ASEAN neighbours – particularly Malaysia and Singapore that have caused a great deal of friction. Indonesia's dispute with Malaysia over the Ambalat waters has already been noted above; which led to a call for Indonesia to downgrade the importance it attaches to ASEAN. With Singapore, the bilateral disputes are broader in scope, covering historical, economic, environmental, territorial, and security-related factors. Singapore is watchful of the political and social upheaval in Indonesia that may affect Singapore itself, as well as the regional stability and prosperity. Singapore was worried about the outbreaks of anti- Chinese rioting of the sort that accompanied the fall of Suharto in 1998, which in its view would undermine "regional stability and has a direct impact on Singapore's wider interests".[35] Economically, the welfare of Indonesian domestic workers in Singapore has been a sore point for Indonesia.

Other issues include the banning of the export of sand to Singapore, which is important for its reclamation projects.[36] It is alleged that the ban, which took effect in 2007 till 2011, was deemed in Singapore to have been politically motivated to secure an extradition treaty with Singapore – another bilateral issue.[37] Also, Indonesia and Singapore are still to complete the finalization of their 1973 maritime boundary agreement by defining unresolved areas north of Indonesia's Batam Island.[38] On security-related issues the dispute has to do with perception from both countries, with Singapore perceiving Indonesia as a haven of Islamic extremists, while the latter perceives the former as a haven of Indonesian corrupt officials and their ill-gotten wealth.[39] More recently tensions flared up in 2014 after the Indonesian military named two of its frigates after the two marines who were convicted in Singapore for bombing a bank building there in March 1965. That incident, which significantly raised tensions between the two countries had been considered closed after Singapore's then Prime Minister Lee Kuan Yew visited the graves of the two marines in Indonesia in 1973. In the recent episode, the commander of TNI was reported by a Singapore newspaper to have apologized for the naming, but he later denied this, saying that he had apologized for not being able to change the naming of the frigates, not for the action itself.

Furthermore, relations between Indonesia and these two neighbours (Malaysia and Singapore) had been affected by the transboundary haze pollution from Indonesia. An episode of haze in 1997 was dubbed as "certainly one of the century's worst environmental disasters", which destroyed an "area the size of Costa Rica".[40] Another severe instance of haze was during the second half of 2006, which prompted Singapore's Prime Minister to write to the Indonesian President expressing his "disappointment" and warning that both ASEAN's credibility, and Indonesia's international standing, would be negatively affected if the problem was not addressed.[41] As with President Suharto in 1997, President Yudhoyono offered an apology and assured of action including ratifying the ASEAN Agreement on Transboundary Haze Pollution signed in 2002. But the Indonesian parliament has refused to ratify the treaty. The recurrence of the haze in June 2013 saw the air pollution index in Singapore and Malaysia reaching an all-time high, and Malaysia declaring a state of emergency in certain affected areas. Indonesia has blamed the haze partly on Singaporean and Malaysian investors who use slash-and-burn techniques for land-clearing.[42] The haze issue has been a contentious issue not only in Indonesia's bilateral ties with Malaysia and Singapore, it also poses a risk of damage to Indonesia's and ASEAN's reputation, although President Yudhoyono has in all sincerity pledged utmost action to reduce the risk of haze.

Bilateral disputes between Indonesia and the Philippines are security-related and territorial in nature. There is an issue of inadequately addressing insurgency-based security threats with regional ramifications on counter-terrorism efforts. As one report put it:

> Despite battling similar security problems, bilateral relations between the Philippines and Indonesia remain distant. The Manila administration's close alignment with the US has in the past prevented bilateral co-operation, despite the regional militant group Jemaah Islamiyah (JI) moving from Indonesia to establish bases on the southern Philippine island of Mindanao. The two countries have tended to blame each other for not adequately addressing security threats, which can be attributed to a large extent to the insurgencies having taken place in areas more or less beyond government control.[43]

Another issue is the maritime dispute between the two countries over waters between Sulawesi and Mindanao.[44]

Asia-Pacific Economic Cooperation (APEC)

APEC was the first intergovernmental regional economic organization among Asia-Pacific countries aimed at promoting trade liberalization. Although formally convened in 1989 in Canberra, APEC was preceded by a number of non-governmental or semi-governmental initiatives, such as the Pacific Economic Cooperation Council (PECC). While these initiatives and ideas behind them were initially proposed and led by experts and officials from Japan, Australia and the US, Indonesia along with other ASEAN countries came to play an important role in APEC. Especially important in this evolutionary stages were Indonesian think-tank experts such as the late Hadi Soesastro.

Indonesia's goal in APEC was to use it for promoting free trade in the region, as well as to ensure a central place for ASEAN countries in managing Asia-Pacific relations. This latter objective was especially important since in the initial stages, the idea of a Pacific economic community, which was the precursor of APEC, was driven by the three developed economies, Australia and the US and its close ally Japan. This risked marginalizing the interests and voice of ASEAN. Indonesia lent support to ASEAN's position that APEC's development should not come at the expense of ASEAN.

Once APEC was formed, Indonesia could play a key role in it. It was at the APEC meeting in Bogor 1994, a year after the grouping was elevated from ministerial to a summit level forum, that "APEC was given the vision that has guided its work and progress to date".[45] As the APEC chairman, Indonesia is credited with helping the Asia-Pacific economies have a common and uniting vision of achieving the Bogor goals, i.e. "commitment to complete the achievement of our goal of free and open trade and investment in the Asia-Pacific no later than the year 2020".[46]

Indonesia hosted the APEC Summit again in 2013. While APEC's importance has declined somewhat in view of the proliferation of bilateral and subregional trade agreements in the region, Indonesia continues to support APEC as providing an opportunity for regional economic cooperation generally, and for its economic development specifically. "For Indonesia, the potential and opportunities for economic cooperation in APEC can be used to increase the Indonesian economic capacity, competitiveness and innovation and encourage the establishment of an open market in Asia Pacific." In June 2013, Ambassador Wahid Supriyadi, Special Advisor to the Minister on Economy, Social and Cultural Issues, highlighted the "strategic positioning" of Indonesia as the host country for APEC 2013. "APEC is a high-level forum that facilitates economic growth, cooperation, trade and investment in the Asia Pacific region."[47] The Ministry of Foreign Affairs saw the meeting as "an opportunity to show Indonesia's active role in promoting regional economic resilience, utilizing regional economic integration for economic growth, creating job and increasing investment and Indonesian export" as to "bring positive benefits for promoting trade, investment, tourism and culture".

ASEAN Regional Forum (ARF)

The ARF was the first truly "multilateral" security forum covering the wider Asia-Pacific region. It is the only "regional" security framework in the world today in which all the major powers (including the US, China, Japan, Russia and India, as well as the European Union) are represented. The ARF is also a rare example of a security institution in which the great power members have willingly conceded leadership and agenda-setting functions to the less powerful developing member states (ASEAN).

Like APEC, the initial proposals for a multilateral security forum in Asia Pacific came from non-Asian states, especially, the then Soviet Union, Canada and Australia. By accepting the ARF, Indonesia had to rethink its policy of keeping outside powers from involvement in Southeast Asia's security affairs. But the ARF was meant to address security challenges in the wider Asia Pacific region, and as with APEC, but to an even greater degree, Indonesia worked to ensure that the development of the ARF does not marginalize ASEAN, but rather gives it a central role in the new forum. The ARF draws upon, and extends, the norms of ASEAN members, including those found in its Treaty of Amity and Cooperation (TAC). Thus, the first meeting of the ARF held in Bangkok in July 1994 saw agreement by the member nations to "endorse the purposes and principles" of the Treaty "as a code of conduct governing relations between states and a unique diplomatic instrument for regional confidence building, preventive diplomacy and political and security cooperation".[48] This principle of ASEAN centrality means that the ARF's annual ministerial meetings are always held in an ASEAN member state, and ASEAN remains in the "driver' seat" of the ARF. The principle of "ASEAN centrality" extends to the Asia-Pacific security architecture generally.

The ARF's initial agenda was defined at its 1995 annual ministerial meeting in Brunei, which called for a three-step approach: confidence-building, preventive diplomacy and "elaboration of approaches to conflicts". Since then, the ARF has moved slowly and cautiously in pursuing this agenda. Its confidence-building measures consist primarily of non-legalistic, non-intrusive, and non-binding measures, such as voluntary statements on national defence postures, meetings among heads of national defence institutions, and exchanges of personnel in key security areas. Its preventive diplomacy agenda has been marked by debate over sovereignty and non-interference. As a result, the ARF's preventive diplomacy concept excludes intra-state conflicts, and it is yet to develop a role in dispute-settlement and conflict resolution. Indonesia has hosted the annual ARF meeting in 2003 and 2011, and plays an important role in its inter-sessional groups. In an important development, the first of the annual ARF Security Policy Conference (ASPC), chaired by Indonesia and hosted by China in Beijing took place on 4–6 November 2004. In 2008, Australia and Indonesia co-organized a Desktop Exercise on Disaster Relief in Jakarta.

Indonesia's agenda in the ARF can be based on the interests it pursues through this ASEAN-led institution. Since the ARF is an ASEAN-led process, it provides a further opportunity for Indonesia, as a leader of ASEAN to project a managerial role in the wider Asia-Pacific region.[49] While the ARF is often criticized as a "talk shop", Indonesia continues to view the forum "as the prime forum for political and security issues in the region", with a "critical role in ensuring a peaceful and stable political and security environment for its people".[50] The ARF conforms to Indonesia's overall approach to regional order, which is driven more through norm-setting and consensus-building than direct problem-solving action.

East Asia Summit (EAS)

The advent of the EAS more generally represented a new stage in the evolution of Asian regionalism and ASEAN. Until 1997, regional institutions in Asia were organised either on a subregional basis (ASEAN being the main example) or a transpacific (APEC and ARF) basis. But the 1997 Asian financial crisis gave an impetus for creating an East Asian (as opposed to Asia-Pacific) framework. The purpose of the EAS, as the (2005) inaugural Kuala Lumpur summit declaration put it, would be to serve as a forum for dialogue on "broad strategic, political and economic issues of common interest and concern".[51] One of the key issues for the EAS was its membership. When it was established in Kuala Lumpur, the EAS consisted of the "ASEAN plus Three" countries (the ten ASEAN members plus China, Japan and South Korea), and three non-East Asian nations: Australia, New Zealand and India. Indonesia had pushed for expanding EAS beyond the narrow geographic scope originally contained in the vision of an East Asia Economic Grouping (EAEG) proposed by Malaysia's former Prime Minister Mahathir Mohammed in the early 1990s. According to Hassan Wirajuda, who was Foreign Minister when the EAS was launched, "Indonesia was the only country other than Singapore which from the start wanted the EAS to be more than ASEAN plus Three". Jakarta wanted to make the EAS broader in order to create a "more balanced, inclusive East Asia". For Indonesia, "East Asia is not a geographic concept". The inclusion of India was especially significant; "India was nowhere before" in the Asia Pacific, and "Indonesia provided a bridge for India to join the EAS."[52]

Indonesia was also one of the key proponents for expanding the EAS to include the US along with Russia, both of which attended the EAS summit for the first time in 2011 (in 2010, the US was represented by Secretary of State, Hillary Clinton).[53] Bob Carr, the former Australian Minister for Foreign Affairs, would describe the EAS Bali Summit in November 2011 with the United States and Russia in attendance for the first time as "a triumph for Indonesia and for the Association of South East Asian Nations (ASEAN)".[54] But the inclusion of the US in the EAS poses a challenge to Indonesia. It has not gone down well with China, which had wanted to keep the EAS an exclusive club of East Asia (ASEAN Plus Three) nations. Moreover, the Obama administration sees its membership in the EAS as an important part of its "pivot" or "rebalancing" policy. This poses a key test of Indonesia's "dynamic equilibrium" concept. Even though Indonesia sought the US participation in the EAS, it would not want to see "too much rebalancing" on the part of the US.[55]

Indonesia does not want to use the EAS to focus exclusively on strategic issues, which is an area stressed by the US. Jakarta sees the EAS "as a forum for dialogue on broad strategic, political and economic issues of common interest and concern with the aim of promoting peace, stability and economic prosperity in East Asia". It also wants to keep the EAS as a leaders-led forum and emphasizes the need for keeping ASEAN "as the driving force" in the EAS.[56]

The inclusion of the US alongside India, in the EAS presents opportunities for Indonesia to pursue its Indo-Pacific normative framework. Indonesia hosted the EAS for the first time in 2011. Indonesia also pushed for an expanded TAC or code of conduct at the 6th EAS held in Bali Indonesia on 19 November 2011. There the leaders adopted the Declaration of the East Asia Summit on the Principles for Mutually Beneficial Relations and committed themselves to the following principles:

- Enhancement of mutual respect for independence, sovereignty, equality, territorial integrity and national identity.

- Respect for international law.

- Enhancement of mutual understanding, mutual trust and friendship.

- Promotion of good neighbourliness, partnership and community building.

- Promotion and maintenance of peace, stability, security and prosperity.

- Non-interference in the internal affairs of another country.

- Renunciation of the threat of use of force or use of force against another state, consistent with the UN Charter.

- Recognition and respect for the diversity of ethnic, religious, cultural traditions and values, as well as diversity of views and positions, including by promoting the voices of moderation.

- Enhancement of regional resilience, including in the face of economic shocks and natural disasters.

- Respect for fundamental freedoms, the promotion and protection of human rights, and the promotion of social justice.

- Settlement of differences and disputes by peaceful means.

- Enhancement of mutually beneficial cooperation in the EAS and with other regional fora.[57]

The South China Sea Conflict

Indonesia does not present itself as a direct party to the South China Sea dispute, (the "recognized" parties to the dispute include China, Taiwan, Malaysia, Brunei, Philippines, and Vietnam). In the 1980s China and Indonesia reached an understanding that they did not have overlapping claims in the South China Sea. But the situation is more ambiguous today. In 2009, China strongly protested Indonesia's arrest of 75 Chinese fishermen near the Natuna islands (a collection of 272 islands at the southern end of the South China Sea in Indonesia's Riau Islands province) on the grounds that they were operating in their "traditional fishing grounds", which brought home to Indonesia's strategic planners the growing Chinese "assertiveness" in the South China Sea.[58] China's nine-dash line map in the South China Sea, which covers the area it claims, overlaps with Indonesian EEZ projected from Indonesia's Natuna Islands. Some observers believe this might affect Indonesia's hitherto status as a non-claimant country which can play the role of an independent mediator.[59] In the meantime, the Indonesian military has publicly declared its intention to pay closer watch over the area and devote more resources,[60] although the Indonesian Defence Minister, Purnomo Yusgiantoro, claims that relations with China are in good shape.[61] There is little question that Indonesia's policymakers are increasingly concerned, at least privately, about the security challenge posed to Indonesia's sovereignty from Chinese encroachments in the South China Sea.

Indonesia has been more publicly concerned with the regional ramifications of the South China Sea conflict, and considers the peaceful management of the dispute as one of the issues of highest importance for regional security. As President Yudhoyono urged in September 2012: "It is...imperative that the potential conflict in the South China Sea be managed with prudence and restraint. It is also vitally important that ASEAN and China very soon conclude a legally binding Code of Conduct of Parties in the South China Sea."[62]

In the 1990s the South China Sea conflict was widely viewed by ASEAN governments as the major "flashpoint of conflict" in post-Cold War Southeast Asia. It also posed a serious test of ASEAN's unity and to its norms concerning the peaceful settlement of disputes. It was Indonesia, and not ASEAN as a group, which took the lead in developing an informal and non-official approach to the conflict in the form of a series of workshops aimed at "managing potential conflicts in the South China Sea". Jakarta, with Canadian support, sought to project its South China Sea initiative as an example of ASEAN's role in regional conflict management.[63] China, Taiwan and Vietnam were not invited to the first Workshop, which focused on developing a common ASEAN position on the issue.[64] This changed at the second Workshop in 1990 in Bandung in July 1991, where the ASEAN six were joined by China, Taiwan, Vietnam and Laos.

The Workshop series deliberately avoided dealing with sensitive territorial issues. Its proponents argued that the holding of the Workshop series was in itself an important confidence-building measure, offering the participants a chance to develop a certain level of transparency regarding national positions on the complex dispute. The series instead concentrated on issues of joint development and functional cooperation, producing agreements on specific projects such as combating marine environmental pollution that might also have a confidence-building effect. The Workshops also explored the task of developing a code of conduct for states of the South China Sea region, with a view to reducing the risk of military conflict among them. Proposals for CBMs, such as non-expansion of military presences in the disputed areas, and exchanges of visits by military commanders in the disputed areas were discussed, but proved elusive with China opposing any discussion of military issues in this forum. Ideas about joint development of resources ran into obstacles, including Beijing's objection to any negotiations involving Taiwan, the unlikely prospect that any of the claimants which already had a military presence on the islands would agree to a withdrawal, and problems in deciding the principles for fair allocation of rights and profit.

Negotiations between China and ASEAN continued, leading in November 2002 to the signing of a "Declaration" on a Code of conduct (DOC) in the South China Sea at the ASEAN summit in Cambodia. The most significant words of the DOC concerned an undertaking by the parties "to exercise self-restraint in the conduct of activities that would complicate or escalate disputes and affect peace and stability including, among others, refraining from action of inhabiting on the presently uninhabited islands, reefs, shoals, cays, and other features and to handle their differences in a constructive manner". The DOC did not include a specific commitment to freeze erection of new structures in the disputed area, a commitment sought by the Philippines, but refused by China.

Jakarta has been worried about the subsequent escalation of the dispute with growing Chinese military assertiveness in the South China Sea. A serious diplomatic test was ASEAN's failure to issue its customary joint communiqué at its last ministerial meeting (ASEAN Ministerial Meeting, or the AMM) in Cambodia held during 9–13 July 2012. The key factor here was Cambodia's refusal to accept language that specifically mentioned the Scarborough Shoal, along with language calling for respect for EEZs and the continental shelf as had been proposed by the Philippines. The Philippines' position, which had the support of other ASEAN members, including Indonesia, was that the Chinese occupation of the Scarborough Shoal and its granting of an oil service contract in the EEZ and continental shelf claimed were gross violations of the DOC, and hence deserved to be mentioned specifically in the communiqué.

As noted, it was Indonesian Foreign Minister Natelagawa who led the damage control effort by making a tour of Manila, Hanoi, Bangkok, Phnom Penh and Singapore. This proved useful in reversing the setback to ASEAN's image to some extent. Moreover, on 20 July, Cambodia as ASEAN Chair, issued a statement containing six principles on the South China Sea on behalf of the ASEAN Foreign Ministers, which reaffirmed ASEAN's commitment to the full implementation of the DOC; Guidelines for the Implementation of the DOC; the early conclusion of a Regional Code of Conduct (COC) in the South China

Sea; full respect of the universally recognized principles of international law including the 1982 UNCLOS; continued exercise of self-restraint and non-use of force by all parties; and peaceful resolution of disputes in accordance with the universally recognized principles of international law including the 1982 UNCLOS.[65]

ASEAN has also managed some concessions from China. China reversed its opposition to ASEAN's right to hold prior consultations among its members before meeting China on the South China Sea issue. In 2012, China dragged its feet on the issue of a binding code of conduct in the South China Sea, insisting that it would sign such a code of conduct only "when conditions are ripe".[66] But in July 2013, at the Brunei ASEAN meeting, China did show more flexibility and agreed to start formal negotiations on the COC.[67] This assuaged ASEAN's concerns to some extent and demonstrated the usefulness of its persistence in holding China accountable to the idea of a COC.

Nevertheless, challenges remain before the conclusion of a COC. Natalegawa cautions that a code "is not a magic wand that will solve the underlying conflict, the territorial disputes. That's for the parties concerned to negotiate." At the same time, he stressed the critical importance of ASEAN unity over the issue, which could not be taken for granted. "As long as ASEAN is united then we will be all right. But as soon as we begin to have an à la carte ASEAN outlook, picking and choosing the piece that we like, that's when things will become more problematic."[68] He wants to "really push hard on the COC", but feels that progress has been slow under the leadership of Thailand, which is currently the country responsible for managing ASEAN's negotiations with China. Indonesia is cautiously optimistic on further progress. Natalegawa sees "more convergence" in the positions of the two sides. Indonesia's goal is to have a COC that contains "actionable steps" including measures aimed at "avoiding and managing incidents", rather than just the "motherhood and apple pie" kind. But getting this type of a binding COC remains far from assured.

Notes

[1]   Ministry of Foreign Affairs, Indonesia <http://www.kemlu.go.id/Pages/IFP.aspx?P=Regional&l=en>

2   J. Soedjati Djiwandono, "The Political and Security Aspects of ASEAN: Its Principal Achievements", *Indonesian Quarterly* 11 (July 1983): 20.

3   Dewi Fortuna Anwar, *Indonesia in ASEAN* (Singapore: Institute of Southeast Asian Studies, 1994), p. 45.

4   Cited in Amitav Acharya, *Constructing a Security Community in Southeast Asia: ASEAN and the Problem of Regional Order,* 2nd edition (Abingdon, Oxford, UK, and New York: Routledge, 2009), p. 74.

5   Adam Malik, "Djakarta Conference and Asia's Political Future", *Pacific Community* 2, no. 1 (October 1970): 74.

6   Adam Malik, "Regional Cooperation in International Politics", in *Regionalism in Southeast Asia* (Jakarta: Centre for Strategic and International Studies,1975), pp. 162–63.

7   Malik, "Regional Cooperation in International Politics", p. 160.

8   Further details of the Indonesian mediation can be found in Acharya, *Constructing a Security Community in Southeast Asia,* pp. 59–61.

9   Amitav Acharya, "Is There a Lack of Focus in Indonesia's Foreign Policy", *The Straits Times,* 2 October 2000.

10 President Yudhoyono, interviewed with the author, Jakarta, 16 January 2014.

11 Indonesian Foreign Ministry, "Towards an ASEAN Security Community", 9 May 2003.

12 Further discussion in Acharya, *Constructing a Security Community in Southeast Asia,* pp. 259–67.

13 Indonesian Foreign Ministry, "Towards an ASEAN Security Community". This formulation and some other phrases in defining a security community were directly derived from the first edition of this author's *Constructing a Security Community in Southeast Asia,* 1st edition (London and New York: Routledge, 2001), pp. 17, 20.

14 Hassan Wirajuda, interview with the author, Jakarta, 12 March 2014.

15 Rizal Sukma, "Indonesia and the Emerging Sino-US Rivalry in Southeast Asia" <http://www.lse.ac.uk/IDEAS/publications/reports/pdf/SR015/SR015-SEAsia-Sukma-.pdf>

16 Rizal Sukma, "Indonesia needs a post-ASEAN foreign policy", *Jakarta Post,* 30 June 2009 <http://www.thejakartapost.com/news/2009/06/30/indonesia-needs-a-postasean-foreign-policy.html>

17 Ibid.

18 Ibid.

19 Rizal Sukma, interview with the author, Jakarta, 10 March 2014.

20 Dewi Fortuna Anwar, " Indonesia's Cautious Confidence", 16 July 2013 <http://www.project-syndicate.org/commentary/asean-and-indonesia-s-foreign-policy-priorities-by-dewi-f-anwar>

21 Pandu Utama Manggala, "Indonesia and the Future of ASEAN Political Security Community" <http://ppia-act.org/2013/08/18/indonesia-and-the-future-of-asean-political-security-community/>

22 Marty Natalegawa, interview with the author, Jakarta, 5 July 2011.

23 Ibid.

24 In 2011, ASEAN Foreign Ministers agreed to deploy military and civilian observers to the troubled border. Both Thailand and Cambodia agreed to permit Indonesian observers to monitor a ceasefire, but the Thai Government, under pressure from its military, subsequently withdrew its support for the mission citing violation of its sovereignty.

25 Marty Natalegawa, interview with the author, Jakarta, 20 January 2014.

26 Donald K. Emmerson, "Indonesia Saves ASEAN's Face", *Asia Times Online*, 24 July 2012 <http://www.atimes.com/atimes/Southeast_Asia/NG24Ae01.html>

27 Marty Natalegawa, interview with the author, Jakarta, 20 January 2014.

28 Hassan Wirajuda, interview with the author, Jakarta 12 March 2014.

29 Ibid.

30 Rafendi Djamin, interview with the author, Washington, D.C., 29 November 2012.

31 Lina Alexandra, "Indonesia's Chairmanship: What are the priorities?" 28 June 2013 <http://www.csis.or.id/post/indonesia%E2%80%99s-chairmanship-what-are-priorities.>

32 Marty Natalegawa, interview with the author, Jakarta, 5 July 2011.

33 Kavi Chongkittavorn, "Indonesia Expands ASEAN's Role", *Asia Pacific Bulletin*, no.111 (19 May 2011) <http://www.eastwestcenter.org/sites/default/files/private/apb111_1.pdf.>

34 Speech by H.E. Dr Susilo Bambang Yudhoyono, President of the Republic of Indonesia, at the Opening Ceremony of the 19th ASEAN Summit, Bali, Indonesia, 17 November 2011 <http://www.asean.org/news/item/speech-he-dr-susilo-bambang-yudhoyono-president-of-the-republic-of-indonesia-at-the-opening-ceremony-of-the-19th-asean-summit>

35 Jane's Sentinel Security Assessment – Southeast Asia, "Singapore – External Affairs", 25 September 2012 <https://janes-ihs-com.proxyau.wrlc.org/CustomPages/Janes/DisplayPage.aspx?DocType=Reference&ItemId=+++1305136&Pubabbrev=SEA>

36 Amitav Acharya, *Constructing a Security Community in Southeast Asia: ASEAN and the Problem of Regional Order*, 3rd edition (London and New York: Routledge, 2014), p. 125.

37 Two quotations from Jane's related to this are: "Indonesia once again banned exports of sand to Singapore, essential for the latter's construction and reclamation projects." The "ban was more openly linked to Jakarta's desire to secure the extradition of suspects alleged to have illegally removed billions of dollars from Indonesia and either invested or held it in Singapore. Indonesian naval vessels enforced the ban, which by June 2011 remained in place." See Jane's

Sentinel Security Assessment – Southeast Asia, "Singapore – External Affairs", 25 September 2012 <https://janes-ihs-com.proxyau.wrlc.org/CustomPages/Janes/DisplayPage.aspx?DocType=Reference&ItemId=+++1305136&Pubabbrev=SEA>

38   Central Intelligence Agency, The World Fact Book. "Dispute – International". <https://www.cia.gov/library/publications/the-world-factbook/fields/2070.html>

39   Jane's Sentinel Security Assessment – Southeast Asia, "Singapore – External Affairs", 25 September 2012 <https://janes-ihs-com.proxyau.wrlc.org/CustomPages/Janes/DisplayPage.aspx?DocType=Reference&ItemId=+++1305136&Pubabbrev=SEA>

40   David Glover and Timothy Jessup, eds., Indonesia's Fires and Haze: The Cost of Catastrophe (Ottawa: International Development Research Centre and Singapore: Institute of Southeast Asian Studies,1999).

41   Jeremy Leong, "Singapore: Review of Major Policy Statements", Singapore Year Book of International Law 11 (2007): 281 <http://law.nus.edu.sg/sybil/downloads/articles/SYBIL–2007/SYBIL–2007–277.pdf>

42   "Singapore hit by highest haze levels in 16 years", 18 June 2013 <http://www.bbc.com/news/world-asia-22935068>

43   Jane's Sentinel Security Assessment – Southeast Asia, "Philippines- External Affairs", 7 February 2014 <https://janes-ihs-com.proxyau.wrlc.org/CustomPages/Janes/DisplayPage.aspx?DocType=Reference&ItemId=+++1305079&Pubabbrev=SEA>

44   Jane's Sentinel Security Assessment – Southeast Asia, "Indonesia – External Affairs", 4 September 2013 <https://janes-ihs-com.proxyau.wrlc.org/CustomPages/Janes/DisplayPage.aspx?DocType=Reference&ItemId=+++1305004&Pubabbrev=SEA>

45   Shiro Armstrong, "Indonesia connects APEC to regional ambitions", East Asian Forum, 6 October 2013. <http://www.eastasiaforum.org/2013/10/06/indonesia-connects-apec-to-regional-ambitions/>

46   1994 Leaders' Declaration, "Bogor Declaration – APEC Economic Leaders' Declaration of Common Resolve", 15 November 1994 <http://www.apec.org/Meeting-Papers/Leaders-Declarations/1994/1994_aelm.aspx>

47   Quoted in "The Role of the Indonesian Government and Business Sector in Leveraging Opportunities in APEC 2013 for Economic Development in Asia Pacific Region", 12 June 2013 <http://www.apec2013ceosummit.com/press/the-role-of-the-indonesian-government-and-business-sector-in-leveraging-opportunities-in-apec-2013-for-economic-development-in-asia-pacific-region.html>

48   "Chairman's Statement: The First Meeting of the ASEAN Regional Forum (ARF), 25 July 1994, Bangkok", p. 2.

49   Ministry of Foreign Affairs of the Republic of Indonesia, "ASEAN Regional Forum" <http://kemlu.go.id/Pages/IFPDisplay.aspx?Name=RegionalCooperation&IDP=5&P=Regional&l=en>

50   ASEAN Regional Forum, Annual Security Outlook 2013 <http://aseanregionalforum.asean.org/files/ARF-Publication/ARF-Annual-Security-Outlook/ARF%20Annual%20Security%20Outlook%202013.pdf>

51 Kuala Lumpur Declaration on the East Asian Summit, Kuala Lumpur, 14 December 2005 <http://www.mofa.go.jp/region/asia-paci/eas/joint0512.html>

52 Hassan Wirajuda, interview with the author, Jakarta, 12 March 2014.

53 According to Ernest Bower of Center for Strategic and International Studies, Washington, D.C. during the "negotiations over the admission of new members to the EAS, Indonesia was a strong supporter of the campaign within ASEAN to have the United States admitted as a full member. This movement, led by Vietnam and Indonesia, defeated a Singaporean initiative to convene a separate, expanded meeting that would have been known as the EAS + 2. This was an effort on Indonesia's part to anchor the United States in regional institutions." Ernest Bower, "Great, but unfocused: Indonesia Assessments of U. S. Power", <https://csis.org/files/publication/110613_bower_CapacityResolve_Web.pdf>

54 Bob Carr, "The East Asia Summit: Building our Regional Arhitecture for the 21st Century", *Strategic Review, The Indonesian Journal of Leadership, Policy and World Affairs,* July 2012 <http://foreignminister.gov.au/articles/2012/bc_ar_120706.html>

55 Marty Natalegawa, interview with the author, Jakarta, 20 January 2014.

56 Chairman's Statement of the 6th East Asia Summit, Bali, Indonesia, 19 November 2011 <http://www.asean.org/images/2013/external_relations/11_chairmans%20statement%20of%20the%206th%20eas.pdf>

57 "Declaration of the East Asia Summit on the Principles for Mutually Beneficial Relations", 19 November 2011 <http://www.asean.org/images/2013/external_relations/eas%20declaration%20of%20principles%2019%20november%202011.pdf>

58 Alan Dupont & Christopher G. Baker, "East Asia's Maritime Disputes: Fishing in Troubled Waters", *The Washington Quarterly* 37, no. 1 (Spring 2014): 85; Remarks by Hassan Wirajuda, Former Foreign Minister of Indonesia, at Brookings Institution, Washington, D.C., 28 April 2014.

59 Ann Marie Murphy, "Jakarta Rejects China's Nine-Dash Line", *Asia Times Online,* 3 April 2014 <http://www.atimes.com/atimes/Southeast_Asia/SEA-01-030414.html>

60 "Indonesia's Military Flexes Muscle as S. China Sea Dispute Looms", *Jakarta Globe,* 13 May 2014 <http://www.thejakartaglobe.com/news/indonesia-military-flexes-muscle-s-china-sea-dispute-looms/.>

61 The Defence Minister told the author that the "Natuna Islands are not an issue with China" and that Indonesia's relations with China are "beautiful", as are relations with the US. Purnomo Yusgiantoro, interview with the author, Jakarta, 16 January 2014.

62 Keynote Address by President Yudhoyono at the Launching of *The Strategic Review Journal* at the Price Waterhouse Coopers Building Auditorium, New York, 26 September 2012 <http://www.embassyofindonesia.org/press/docpdf/Speech-President-SBY-Strategic%20Review%20Launch.pdf>

63 J. Soedjati Djiwandono, Preface to Special Issue on "South China Sea: Views from ASEAN", *Indonesian Quarterly* 18, no. 2 (1990): 102.

64 Ambassador Hasjim Djalal, "Territorial Disputes at Sea: Situation, Possibilities, Progress", Paper presented to the 10th Asia Pacific Roundtable, Kuala Lumpur, 5–8 June 1996, pp. 2–3.

[65] Carlyle A. Thayer, "ASEAN's Code of Conduct in the South China Sea: A Litmus Test for Community-Building?" *Asia-Pacific Journal* 10, no. 4 (20 August 2012) <http://www.japanfocus.org/-Carlyle_A_-Thayer/3813>

[66] Dario Agnote, "ASEAN needs 'more effective' code with China on Sea row", ABS-CNB News, 7 October 2013 <http://www.abs-cbnnews.com/focus/07/10/13/asean-needs-more-effective-code-china-see-row>

[67] "Remarks by Foreign Minister Yang Jiechi at the ARF Foreign Ministers' Meeting", <http://www.fmprc.gov.cn/eng/zxxx/t842183.htm>

[68] Marty Natalegawa, interview with the author, Jakarta, 20 January 2014.

Chapter 4

INDONESIA AND
THE MAJOR POWERS

Indonesia's relations with the major powers in the Asia-Pacific (a term which will be used in this chapter despite the growing currency of the term "Indo-Pacific" in recent years) are an important basis of its role as an emerging power. Strategically positioned in the Asia-Pacific region containing some of the most economically and militarily powerful actors of the century and considered to be the strategic hub of the 21st century world order, Indonesia has seized the opportunity of developing closer ties with the powers of the Asia-Pacific. Doing so allows it a role not only in shaping the regional architecture of the Indo-Pacific, but also and by implication, in the evolving world order in general. Thus, by developing close bilateral ties with the major powers, Indonesia can be seen as shooting two birds with one stone: bolstering its role in the regional architecture and developing a greater role in the world order and global governance.

From an Indonesian perspective the most important Asia-Pacific powers are the US, China, Japan, Australia, and India. Although both Russia and the EU figure in Indonesia's strategic calculations (Russia is a major arms supplier to Indonesia and the EU countries are economic partners as well as a source of arms) they are not viewed to be as critical to shaping the regional balance of power as the others.

While Indonesia does not regard itself as a major or "great" power in the traditional sense of the term, it has the distinction of enjoying good relations with all the major powers in the Asia-Pacific. Indeed, it may be the only sizeable regional player to be in such a position. Another striking feature is that of all the major regional powers, Indonesia has a strong relationship with China. Moreover, Indonesia's relationship with these powers, especially the US, has not only experienced a dramatic turnaround in the post-Suharto era, but has also broadened to include cooperation on regional and global issues of mutual concern. Jakarta has developed "comprehensive" and "strategic" partnerships with all of them.[1]

After the fall of Suharto in 1998, Indonesia's relations with the US suffered a setback with the violence in East Timor in 1999 leading to a cut-off of US arms supplies to Indonesia. But ties strengthened as the democratization and reform process took hold in Indonesia, culminating in the November 2010 signing of the Indonesia-US Comprehensive Partnership. The agreement provided for high-level engagement and cooperation under three pillars: political and security, economic and development, and sociocultural, educational, science and technology.

Successive US Presidents have endorsed and enthused about Indonesia's potential and democratic progress. In 2006, President George W. Bush stated: "It's very important for the people of America to understand that this vast country has got not only tremendous potential, but it's got a prominent role to play in the world."[2] And at a speech during his visit to Indonesia in November 2010, President Obama stressed that the US-Indonesia partnership "is a partnership of equals, grounded in mutual interests and mutual respect".[3]

US leaders have often pointed to Indonesia's democratic transition as the basis of a new relationship. Shortly after assuming her position as Secretary of State, Hillary Clinton visited Jakarta and spoke of the two countries' shared "commitment to democratic values, human rights, and a vibrant civil society".[4] For their part, Indonesia's leaders have also stressed shared values as the core of the new relationship. Foreign Minister Marty Natalegawa told a Washington, D.C. audience in 2010 that: "Today, the United States and Indonesia are respectively the second and the third largest democracies in the world – which means that we are both totally committed to the same values and ideals, including those enshrined in the UN Charter."

This is not to say that the US attitude towards Indonesia is based purely on shared values. Strategic considerations, especially the rise of China, also play a major part. A senior Western diplomat with considerable experience in US-Indonesian ties says that "Indonesia is the only country in Asia Pacific which, I won't say it can stand up to China, but at least cannot be pressured into accommodating China. It has the mass, credibility to do this. Hence an independent, strong Indonesia is in US interest."[5] The US also sees Indonesia as a key player in ensuring maritime security in the region, especially in the

Malacca, Sunda and Lombok Straits through which pass "close to half of the global merchant fleet capacity".[6] Indonesia's strategic importance to the US interest in the freedom of navigation in the region has intensified against the backdrop of Chinese assertiveness in the South China Sea. Another basis of the strengthened relations is their shared membership in regional institutions, including APEC, the ARF and EAS, which both (although Indonesia to a greater extent than the US) see as the anchor of regional stability. Another area of US strategic interest in Indonesia is the global war on terror. The US has found it useful to court the support of the largest Muslim-majority nation in fighting terrorism – building on the past support of President Megawati Sukarnoputri to President Bush's US war on terror in 2001.

Both American and Indonesian leaders see their relationship going beyond a strictly bilateral level to cover wider regional and global issues.[7] A US "fact sheet" on the US-Indonesia relations claims that the two countries "consult regularly on issues such as humanitarian assistance and disaster relief, climate change, and the spread of communicable diseases" as well as "the three pillars of the Nuclear Nonproliferation Treaty – nonproliferation, peaceful uses of nuclear energy, and disarmament".[8] The two countries do not necessarily have similar positions on global governance issues and the reform of global institutions. For example, Indonesia's position on the US intervention in Iraq in 2003 was sharply critical of the US. Its stance on humanitarian interventions in Libya and Syria has differed from that of the US. Nonetheless, Indonesian leaders have treaded cautiously on the subject of America's leadership in addressing global challenges such as terrorism, climate change, etc. As President Yudhoyono put it in 2008 while addressing the issue of leadership in the world:

> None of these global challenges can be addressed by the world community without having America on-board. And conversely, none of these issues can be resolved by the United States alone.[9]

A watershed in the bilateral relations between Indonesia and the US was marked by President Barack Obama's visit to Indonesia on 9–10 November 2010 in which the presidents of both countries officially launched the Indonesia-US Comprehensive Partnership (CP). Before the launching, bilateral relations had been implemented through the first Indonesia-United States Joint Commission Meeting (JCM) in Washington, D.C. on 17 September 2010 which was moderated by the Foreign Ministers of both countries. Economic ties between the two countries remain relatively insignificant, however. The US is the 4th biggest trading partner of Indonesia after Japan, China and Singapore with total trade amounting to US$23 billion in 2010.[10] US foreign direct investment (FDI) in Indonesia expanded to US$1.5 billion in 2011, making the United States the third largest foreign investor in Indonesia after Singapore and Britain. More advanced is the defence and security strategic relationship. This has undergone a major shift, after coming to a standstill during the East Timor crisis in 1999. In November 2005, the Bush Administration, citing "national security interests", waived restrictions imposed by Congress on the provision of Foreign Military Financing (FMF) and defence exports to Indonesia. There were no further legislative restrictions on military relations specific to Indonesia. A joint statement by President Bush and President Yudhoyono in May 2006 noted that "normal military relations would be in the interest of both countries". In 2006, the US resumed International Military Education and Training (IMET) aid, enabling some Indonesian military officers to train under the programme. In resuming arms sales and normal defence relations, the Bush Administration stressed Indonesia's importance as "the world's third largest democracy", as "the world's most populous majority-Muslim nation", having a "unique strategic role in Southeast Asia", and playing a key role as "a voice of moderation in the Islamic world". Indonesia was also cited for its "key role in guaranteeing security in the strategic sea lanes in Asia" and as "a leading member of the Association of Southeast Asian Nations". The US noted "significant progress in advancing its democratic institutions and practices in a relatively short time".[11] IMET funds to Indonesia jumped from $938,000 in FY 2006 to $1.5 million in FY2009 (74 students). The US and Indonesia have conducted a number of exercises, such as Garuda Shield 2007, their first joint brigade-size since 1997, and Naval Engagement Activity (NEA) with marines. Also, Indonesia was invited to participate in the Cobra Gold exercise for the first time in 2006.[12] Not all of these relate to the war on terror, though. In appealing to the US Congress to lift military sanctions against Indonesia, Admiral William Fallon, Commander of the US Pacific Command argued: "We cannot afford to cede influence to other regional powers, such as China, with this important country."[13] Further, the two countries have conducted more joint humanitarian relief exercises with other countries in the region. Moreover, in 2012 the Department of State's

Anti-terrorism Assistance programme provided training and equipment to 545 Indonesian police officers. Indonesia and the United States have been organizing annual military meetings since 2002. The meetings have included the Indonesia-United States Security Dialogue (IUSSD) and the United States-Indonesia Bilateral Defense Dialogue (USIBDD) which interspersed with the IUSSD. US arms transfers to Indonesia resumed, including provision of advanced fighter aircraft such as the 24 surplus F-16s announced in 2012.[14]

But the US-Indonesian relationship is not free from challenges. Former Foreign Minister Hassan Wirajuda tells the story of a telephone call he received from US Secretary of State Colin Powell shortly after the US invaded Iraq in 2003. Jakarta had "strongly condemned US military aggression in Iraq", as he put it. Not only was the US action seen as contrary to international law, but Indonesia also worried that the Iraq invasion "might be seen as war between West and Islam". When Powell "called me on the phone", Wirajuda remembers, he "tried to persuade Indonesia to take sides", meaning of course the US side. But he told Powell that Indonesia's position was "not just the government's position, but also that of the civil society and the people". He told Powell: "We are a democracy," to which Powell replied: "As democracies, let's agree to disagree."[15]

That was an unusual case. Relations with the US recovered at the official level and some of the anti-Americanism created by the Iraq invasion was countered by the massive US humanitarian aid for Indonesia in the wake of the Indian Ocean tsunami in late December 2004. But irritants have persisted. From the US perspective, human rights violations in Indonesia have been a major concern of the US Congress.[16] After the Cold War, congressional views on Indonesia were more influenced by ongoing concerns over alleged human rights abuses by the Indonesian National Defence Forces (TNI). The events of 9/11 added the concern of how best to pursue the war against terror in Southeast Asia. Some members of Congress remain dissatisfied with progress on bringing to justice Indonesian military personnel and police responsible for past human rights abuses in East Timor and West Papua. Within Indonesia, there remains a lingering element of suspicion of America's interests and role.[17] This relates to US interference in Indonesia's first national elections in 1955, support for an armed anti-Communist rebellion in Sumatra and Sulawesi during 1957–58, and its support for the Suharto regime.[18]

China

Chinese leaders have recognized Indonesia's strategic importance and role in world affairs. In the words of former Chinese Premier Wen Jiabao: "Indonesia has significant influence in the world...China places great importance on Indonesia's standing and role in international and regional affairs."[19] Aside from their bilateral ties, shared membership in regional and global institutions such as ARF, EAS, APEC, G-20, UN, World Bank, IMF, and WTO has increased opportunities for coordination and cooperation. Indonesia has sought to develop closer ties with China by giving a "strategic orientation" to the ties. According to a report from Singapore's Ministry of Defence such a relationship is guided by four considerations from the Indonesian side: managing its territorial dispute with China over the Natuna Islands, ensuring that the US influence in Southeast Asia does not become too dominant, allowing Indonesia to take leadership in handling ASEAN's relations with China, and benefitting from economic ties with China as well as securing Chinese diplomatic support in pursuit of its international objectives.[20] These considerations are consistent with Indonesia's "dynamic equilibrium" approach, and although their realization is not easy, especially addressing the Natuna Islands issues, they have been followed by Jakarta fairly consistently.

Two-way trade between the two countries has grown swiftly. By 2011, China had become Indonesia's second largest trading partner.[21] Bilateral trade reached US$66.2 billion in 2012 and the two countries set a target of US$80 billion for 2015.[22] At the same time, Indonesia's misgivings about China's long-term strategic ambitions in Asia have grown, in keeping with China's increasing assertiveness in the South China Sea. As discussed in Chapter 3, Jakarta is becoming more worried about Chinese claims to its Natuna Islands. Indicative of Jakarta's discomfort over Chinese policies is the warning issued by Foreign Minister Marty Natalegawa to China in February 2014 (shortly after a visit by US Secretary of State John Kerry to Jakarta) against establishing an Air Defence Identification Zone in the South China Sea, similar to one that Beijing established in 2013 in the East China Sea. As he put it, "We have firmly told China we will not accept a similar zone if it is adopted in the South China Sea."[23] The two countries have also differed on the modalities for developing the Asia-Pacific regional security architecture, with China preferring the ASEAN+3 framework as the modality through which to build an East Asian community, while Indonesia prefers an expanded EAS with the inclusion of the US, Australia and India, as the best way forward.

Australia

Indonesia's relations with Australia confront a different set of problems. During his visit in Indonesia in 1994 when the country was still under Suharto rule, Australian Prime Minister Paul Keating stated that: "No country is more important to Australia than Indonesia. If we fail to get this relationship right, and nurture and develop it, the whole web of our foreign relations is incomplete..."[24] In October 2013, the newly elected Australian Prime Minister Tony Abbott famously said that his foreign policy will be "more Jakarta, less Geneva". As he put it:

> I'm here in Jakarta within two weeks of being sworn in as prime minister because of the importance I place on the relationship between two great neighbours and two major economies. Australia currently has more significant economic relationships – but we have no more important overall relationship because of Indonesia's size, proximity and potential. Indonesia is a member of the G20 and a leader of ASEAN as well as Australia's most important neighbour. It's the world's most populous Muslim nation. It's the world's third largest democracy. And along with India, it's the emerging democratic superpower of Asia.[25]

In reality, Indonesia and Australia have had a volatile "love-hate relationship". After the fall of Sukarno, relations improved under the new leadership of Suharto until 1975 when Australia opposed the Indonesian invasion of East Timor in 1975. In October 1978, Australia offered de facto recognition of Indonesian authority in East Timor. But the crisis in East Timor in 1999 soured the relationship again, with Indonesia abrogating the 1995 security agreement. The terrorist incidents targeting Australians in 2002 Bali bombing and 2003 Marriott Hotel bombing prompted cooperation between the two countries, which was further improved in 2004 when Australia offered assistance after the 2004 Indian Ocean earthquake and tsunami hit Indonesia. In 2006, the Lombok Treaty was signed, a security agreement covering defence, law enforcement, counter-terrorism, intelligence, maritime security, aviation safety, WMD non-proliferation, and bilateral nuclear cooperation for peaceful purposes. In March 2010, President Yudhoyono was invited to address the Australian Parliament. He and the Australian Government agreed to upgrade the relationship to a "comprehensive strategic partnership". In November 2011, Prime Minister Julia Gillard visited Indonesia and formally negotiated the Australia-Indonesia Comprehensive Economic Partnership Agreement (CEPA). In November 2013, the "spying controversy" broke out. Allegations that the Australian Signals Directorate was involved in monitoring the mobile phone calls of President Yudhoyono, his wife, and high-ranking officials, became another low point in the bilateral relations.

In April 2013, then Australian Defence Minister Stephen Smith described Indonesia as "a nation [that is] now taking on a key leadership role in our region and on the global stage. Australia strongly supports such a leadership role for Indonesia".[26] Smith argued that the "relationship between Australia and Indonesia has never been stronger".[27] This is evident in Prime Minister Julia Gillard and President Yudhoyono meeting a minimum of four times per year, not to mention, the frequent meetings at the foreign and defence ministers' level. Indonesia had been the largest ODA recipient from Australia, receiving some AU$462 million during 2008–09, a substantial portion of Australia's total aid budget total AU$3.7 billion.[28] But Australia-Indonesia bilateral trade had fared less well: at a mere US$6.7 billion in 2009, it was growing at a much lower rate than Australia's trade with ASEAN.[29]

In terms of security cooperation, Indonesia has signed strategic partnership and security cooperation agreements with Australia. But theirs is not a security alliance, though still important. The 2008 Agreement on the Framework for Security Cooperation – or the Lombok Treaty – is considered by Indonesia in the words of President Yudhoyono himself, as a "landmark" and a "paradigm shift on the notions of security, threats, mutual respect and cooperation", because it gives Indonesia an Australian commitment to non-interference in its domestic affairs. "That means each side will in no way support any separatist movement against the other."[30]

Indonesian leaders have recognized the importance of the Indonesia-Australia relationship. President Yudhoyono called it a "special relationship" that has "gone through many ups and downs, many generational changes, many political eras, and many crises".[31] He underscored the shared commitment of both countries to "foster a more democratic world order" and both of them being "firm believers in the virtue of multilateralism and in the need to reform the United Nations system". Australia has been a major supporter of the Bali Democracy Forum, which Australia recognizes as "the only intergovernmental forum in Asia on the issue of democracy".[32] Close cooperation also developed in the fight against terrorism including intelligence sharing and information exchange, and capacity building.

In reality, Indonesia's relationship with Australia has never been smooth. A striking summary of the challenges can be found in President Yudhoyono's speech to the Australian Parliament in March 2010, where he highlighted the perception gap that exists between the two countries.

> I was taken aback when I learned that in a recent Lowy Institute survey, 54 percent of Australian respondents doubted that Indonesia would act responsibly in its international relations. Indeed, the most persistent problem in our relations is the persistence of age-old stereotypes – misleading, simplistic mental caricatures that depict the other side in a bad light. Even in the age of cable television and internet, there are Australians who still see Indonesia as an authoritarian country, or as a military dictatorship, or as a hotbed of Islamic extremism, or even as an expansionist power. On the other hand, in Indonesia, there are people who remain afflicted with Australia phobia, those who believe that the notion of "White Australia" still persists, that Australia harbors ill intentions towards Indonesia, and is either sympathetic or supports separatist elements in our country.... I want all Australians to know that Indonesia is a beautiful archipelago, but we are infinitely more than a beach playground with coconut trees.[33]

The issue of people smuggling has been especially divisive. Indonesia and Australia recognize that "people smuggling is a regional problem that requires a regional solution, involving the origin, transit and destination countries to work together", and have worked to develop a "mechanism of cooperation to deal with this issue so that future people-smuggling cases can be handled in a predictable and coordinated way".[34] But there have been problems. Aimed at the cessation of asylum-seeking in Australian borders, the policy of "Operations Sovereign Borders" – an election campaign policy of Tony Abbott which was implemented on 13 September 2013 soon after he was appointed Prime Minister – has caused serious strains in bilateral ties.[35] Indonesia has accused Australia of violating its territorial integrity during Australia's "tow-back operations".[36] Compounding the people-smuggling issue is the espionage scandal in November 2013 when Indonesian officials downgraded the relationship after Prime Minister Abbott refused to apologize for the alleged spying. President Yudhoyono's comments were sharp: "I find it personally hard to comprehend why the tapping was done. We are not in a cold war era… I know Indonesians are upset and angry over what Australia has done to Indonesia. Our reactions will determine the future of the relationship and friendship between Indonesia and Australia – which actually have been going well."[37] Prime Minister Abbott expressed his regret for the embarrassment to the Indonesian President and the country but did not apologize, calling it "reasonable intelligence-gathering activities".[38]

Japan

Indonesia's bilateral ties with Japan are in better shape. Prime Minister Junichiro Koizumi visited the country four times after the 1997 economic crisis. Both countries have been deepening their economic cooperation, especially in trade.[39] Bilateral trade reached US$53 billion in 2011,[40] Indonesia is major supplier of raw materials to Japan and from 1990 to 2009, Japan had invested US$21.6b in Indonesia, making it the top investor.[41] Indonesia is also the largest recipient of Japanese ODA which has financed a large part of its infrastructure in Indonesia. As a leading Indonesian economist put it "Indonesia's development today cannot be explained without Japanese assistance to Indonesia".[42]

In the past, some Indonesian analysts felt that Japan should be more supportive of Indonesia's leadership role in ASEAN in order for both countries to play a greater role in East Asia and beyond. "Japan," argued Jusuf Wanandi, a top Indonesia analyst, "should be more forthcoming in assisting and supporting Indonesia's capabilities for leadership in ASEAN."[43] They also complained of Japan's failure to put its economy and domestic politics in order,[44] and expressed concerns about protectionism in its agriculture, restrictions on technology transfer to Indonesia and on labour movement from Indonesia to Japan. It remains to be seen how Japan's more assertive foreign policy in Southeast Asia would alter such perceptions. Japan's support for Indonesia's political role in the region was highlighted by Prime Minister Hatoyama serving as Co-Chair of the Bali Democracy Forum (BDF) in 2009.[45] Strategic cooperation has also been improving. Their convergence of strategic interest was also indicated when the two countries worked together to expand the membership of the EAS beyond the East Asian region, thereby defying China's wishes. Japan needs Indonesia's support for the Abe government's policy to develop a more forward defence strategy in response to the perceived threat from China. In October 2013, Abe visited Jakarta to explain his security policy. Japan has accepted Indonesia's cherished principle of "ASEAN Centrality" and backed Indonesia's efforts to conclude a code of conduct in the South China Sea on the basis of international law.

India

In 1993, India's "Look East Policy" led to a new momentum in Indonesia-India relations. Indonesia's consent was important for India gaining membership in the ARF and later the EAS. In 2005, during President Yudhoyono's visit to India, both heads of state signed a Strategic Partnership agreement. President Yudhoyono was given the singular honour of being invited as the chief guest of India's Republic Day celebrations in January 2011. Security cooperation between the two countries has also improved, with terrorism being a key issue. Maritime security, especially in the Indian Ocean, is another important issue of cooperation between the two countries.The Indian analyst C. Raja Mohan argues that the relationship between India and Indonesia is being placed on a new basis as each country leaves behind the North-South divide as the main basis of its foreign policy and embraces a new role as "potential consensus-builders" on the world stage through their membership in the G-20. Both countries now stress their credentials as democratic nations, and both have a major role to play in shaping the Asia-Pacific balance of power. Adding to this is the emerging notion of an "Indo-Pacific Region". India's desire to raise its profile in the Pacific part of the "Indo-Pacific" would require Indonesia's political support, and if successful, "end the artificial separation between the two oceans and help construct a new Indo-Pacific region".[46]

Yet, there remains also the possibility that the Indo-Pacific concept might engender a degree of competition. India and Indonesia have yet to tap their bilateral defence cooperation, owing to their differing calculus of strategic interests of both, with Indonesia putting more strategic importance on the Pacific Ocean than the Indian Ocean.[47] Another area that complicates the relationship is the China factor. The extent to which China poses a challenge to the strategic interests of Indonesia and India has a bearing on their bilateral relations. The Joint Statement on the India-Indonesia Strategic Partnership released on 11 October 2013 did not mention China; analysts attribute this to Indonesia's cautious approach to China, and its desire not to be seen as siding with India in its competition with China.[48] Indian maritime doctrine's declaration that the Indian Ocean region, from the Persian Gulf to the Straits of Malacca, is its "legitimate area of interest", might raise concerns in Indonesia. India's Maritime Strategy document released in 2009 listed the Sunda and Lombok straits as falling within the Indian Navy's area of strategic interest. It did note, however, that "cooperation with Indonesia is a prerequisite to enable the navy's operations in these waters".[49]

Despite persistent problems and challenges in its bilateral relations with the major powers (especially China and Australia), Indonesia's overall relationship with them remains positive. It not only complements Jakarta's desire to play a leading role in crafting the Asia-Pacific and Indo-Pacific security architecture, but also underpins its aspirations to enhance its role in global governance.

Indonesia's Military Capacity

Military capacity is traditionally a major component of a country's power. Since the end of the Cold War, Asia has seen an intensified military build-up, with China, Japan, India as well as South Korea and Singapore leading the way. China has undertaken annual double-digit growth in defence spending. Its military spending rose by 175 per cent in real terms between 2003 and 2012.[50] Japan is undertaking extensive military modernization in response to the perceived threat from China. Among the top military spenders in the world in 2012, three Asian nations, China, Japan and India were in 2nd, 5th and 8th place respectively, followed by South Korea in 12th place.[51] And the five biggest importers in the world during the 2008–12 period were all Asian nations: India, China, Pakistan, South Korea and Singapore, in that order.[52]

During the period 2003–12, Indonesia increased its defence spending by nearly 73 per cent.[53] But Indonesia's overall defence spending and arms purchases pale by comparison with the other Asian emerging powers. Indonesia's military capacity and strategy is shaped by its perceived security challenges which have been traditionally focused on internal threats. While transnational and maritime

Table 4.1
Indonesia's Defence Spending 2003–12

Year	2003	2004	2005	2006	2007	2008	2009	2010	2011	2012
Rupiah (trillion)	18.2	21.4	23.9	23.6	32.6	32.8	33.6	42.9	51.1	72.5
US$ (billion)	2.12	2.39	2.47	2.59	3.57	3.40	3.25	4.70	5.82	7.74
Real Growth (%, US$)	33.0	13.0	3.0	5.0	38.0	–5.0	–4.0	45.0	24.0	33.0
Percentage of GDP (US$)	0.99	0.93	0.88	0.75	0.82	0.67	0.60	0.67	0.69	0.86

Source: Figures based on International Institute for Strategic Studies, *The Military Balance*, 2003 to 2013, as presented in Benjamin Schreer, "Moving beyond ambitions? Indonesia's military modernization" (Canberra: Australian Strategic Policy Institute, November 2013), <https://www.aspi.org.au/publications/moving-beyond-ambitions-indonesias-military-modernisation/Strategy_Moving_beyond_ambitions.pdf> (p.16). Reproduced with permission from the author.

security threats have become increasingly more important and while Indonesia has been seeking to enhance its external defence capabilities, there remain important limits to its ability to project power beyond its frontiers. This has partly to do with the political importance of the Army, the principle of territorial defence, and budget constraints and the related lack of modern weapons.

Table 4.1 shows increases in Indonesia defence spending. While spending has risen from US$2.12 billion in 2003 to US$7.74 billion in 2012 amounting to a real growth of 33 per cent, it remains quite low as a percentage of GDP: less than 1 per cent.

Indonesia's strategic planners do not foresee the prospects for any outright invasion of the country. Moreover, the country's defence strategy continues to reflect the primacy of its territorial defence, and the total people's war (*hankamrata*) concepts.[54] A new defence doctrine issued in January 2008, continues to demonstrate a continuing emphasis on internal threats.[55] The Army, politically still the most important arm of the services, comprises over 75 per cent of all three services combined.[56] Indonesia's defence modernization is thus partly geared to improving the capability to address threats of domestic terrorism and separatism. Its armed forces have developed "rapid deployment forces" that could be deployed against domestic threats.

But Indonesia's threat perceptions are increasingly cognizant of the external environment. According to its Ministry of Defence, "The unstable situation in the SCS (South China Sea) and Asia-Pacific could be a threat to Indonesia as well as conflicts among countries in the region."[57] As a vast archipelago of over 13,000 islands with a coastline of 54,716 kilometers, and as a country straddling three of the world's critical chokepoints in the straits of Malacca, Lombok and Sunda,[58] maritime security concerns are important in Indonesia's security perceptions and defence planning. Such concerns include piracy and possible terrorist attacks on these critical sea lanes. Natural disasters are another source of strategic attention. Moreover, Indonesia has had maritime territorial disputes with Malaysia, and concerns about the protection of its extensive exclusive economic zones (EEZs) have led to a greater awareness of the need for enhancing the country's naval capability.

A good deal of Indonesia's recent and ongoing defence spending and force modernization efforts are "catching up efforts" and geared to overcoming severe problems of military equipment obsolescence and lack of readiness.[59] In 2007, a senior Indonesian military official described its force readiness to be at 75 per cent for the Army, less than 50 per cent for the Navy and less than 50 per cent for the Air Force.[60] As one observer puts it, "Among East Asian countries, the ability of Indonesia's defence force to address security challenges, especially the regional ones, is considered one of the weakest."[61] Hence:

> The main objectives of Indonesian force modernization are upgrading military capabilities on the ground and air-sea battle. Replacing obsolete weapon system and upgrading current weapon system, Indonesian military will reach Minimum Essential Force at the latest on 2025.[62] [sic]

The MEF refers to a phased defence modernization programme launched under President Yudhoyono. The MEF "establishes in military terms the number, scale and nature of operational readiness and force structure that the country should be able to deploy at a minimum".[63] Presidential Directive No. 7 of 2008 defined the MEF concept as "a force level that can guarantee the attainment of immediate strategic defence interests, where the procurement priority is given to the improvement of minimum defence strength and/or the replacement of outdated main weapon systems/equipment".[64] The MEF development programme is being implemented in three stages (2010–14, 2015–19, and 2019–24). For the first stage, Indonesia has allocated a budget of US$16 billion, but the Defence Ministry considers this as inadequate, "well below the world defence spending average of around 2.5% of GDP". It hopes that "for the following strategic planning stages the same, or even increased, amount of budget provision could be made available".[65]

Through the MEF, Indonesia aims to address its equipment problems of its armed forces. Although the Army remains important, more attention is being given to the equipment needs of the Navy and the Air Force. Among Indonesia's major recent arms equipment purchases (some of which are being financed by bank loans) are:[66]

- Three Chang Bogo-class attack submarines from South Korea announced in 2012, valued at US$1 billion, the first to be built in South Korea with Indonesian engineers on site, part of the second to be built in Indonesia, and the third to be built by state company PAL in Surabaya.[67]

- 25 Bell 412 utility helicopters for the Army.

- 24 secondhand F-16 C/D fighters from the US. The fighters are given free by the US, but would be upgraded at a cost of US$750 million through the US Foreign Military Sales programme. The deal was agreed in November 2011, and comprises 19 single-seaters and five dual-seaters, with the first four aircraft due in mid-2014, followed by four every three months.[68]

- A programme to jointly build fighter jets (KFX) with South Korea.

- 103 overhauled Leopard 2A6 main battle-tanks from Germany.[69]

- 42 upgraded Marder 1A2 infantry fighting vehicles from Germany.

- Four Sigma-class corvettes ordered from the Netherlands in 2004 for US$1.9 billion.[70]

- Two Sigma 10514 PKR Frigates from the Netherlands, which will be built in both the Netherlands and Surabya.[71]

- Three frigates from Britain.[72]

- The Indonesian Navy (Tentera Nasional Indonesia – Angkatan Laut: TNI-AL) will equip a total of four Ahmad Yani (Van Speijk)-class guided missile frigates and one Kapitan Pattimura (Parchim I)-class corvette with low-probability-of-intercept (LPI) naval radars. <http://www.janes.com/article/36710/indonesia-equips-frigates-corvette-with-stealth-radars>

- Eight Boeing AH-64E Apache attack helicopters valued at US$500 million from the US.

- Since 2003, Indonesia has been purchasing Russian Sukhoi fighters. Its Air Force has SU-27SK, 3 SU-27SKM, 2 SU-30MK, and 9 SU-30MK2.[73] It is reportedly considering buying Russia's Sukhoi Su-35 multi-role fighter to replace its aging Northrop F-5 Tiger fighter jets.[74]

- Eight Embraer Super Tucanoclose-air-support aircraft from Brazil (ordered in November 2010). A contract for a second batch of eight aircraft was announced on 10 July 2012, with deliveries expected in 2014.

- 16 T-50i light attack aircraft worth US$400 million from South Korea, with delivery completed in 2014.[75]

Indonesia does not have any plan to develop a blue water navy for power projection which would require a number of ocean-going ships with logistical support. Its naval modernization instead seeks to develop a "Green-water" navy, which is "a navy that focuses primarily on defending and controlling its oceanic littoral as well as coastal waters, ports and harbours".[76] Whereas a blue water navy requires a capacity for power projection through acquisition of large platforms such as aircraft carriers, and destroyers, etc., a brown water navy focuses on anti-access and area denial with the help of anti-ship missiles, fast attack craft, submarines, shore-launched missiles, land-based tactical fighter aircraft, sea mining and amphibious warfare assets. The objective is to create a credible risk to any potential adversary should it launch a major naval attack against Indonesia.[77] The Indonesian Navy's goal is to develop a 274-ship force by 2024, consisting of 110 surface combatants, 66 patrol vessels and 98 support ships. It also seeks to operate 12 new diesel–electric submarines. As noted above, in 2012 Indonesia signed an agreement with South Korea to acquire three attack submarines,[78] and is reportedly considering buying Kilo-class submarines from Russia.[79]

Even then, according to one assessment published by the Australian Strategic Policy Institute, the navy would have significant limitations in "critical areas such as long-range maritime surveillance, anti-submarine warfare (ASW) and mining/countermining", and would be "far from being able to control most of its territorial waters effectively". And it would lack any "significant maritime power projection capability".[80] But there is another dimension to Indonesia's military modernization and maritime strategy that is often understated, but which gives an important military dimension to its role as an emerging

Asian power. This has to do with its intent to develop a credible capacity for protecting and securing the sealanes and navigation channels that pass through its archipelagic waters. Although the international law of the sea allows passage of military ships and submarines through these waters, Indonesia acts as the guardian of these sealanes. According to Defence Minister Purnomo Yusgiantoro, while "there are no international waters in Indonesia, Indonesia has to allow international passage. Indonesia is responsible for the protection of these sealanes, including deep water passages [likely to be used by foreign submarines] such as in the Arafura Sea. Hence Indonesia needs a strong navy."[81] He sees the importance of the Indonesian Navy not only in terms of ensuring that foreign ships and submarines passing through the international straits do not intrude into Indonesian waters, but also as a kind of regional and international public good. Hence, while Indonesia may not have blue-water ambitions, it can affect naval deployments in the Indo-Pacific region, including the power projection missions of Asian powers such as China, Japan, India, by developing a capacity for policing the international channels that pass through the archipelago.

Indonesia procures much of its military equipment from foreign sources. Its defence acquisition programme is diversified with US, France, Germany, Russia and UK being the major suppliers. The Yudhoyono government has sought to revive Indonesia's domestic procurement programme from the state-owned domestic aviation and defence industry which in recent years has supplied indigenously-built APCs and a limited number of CN235-220 maritime patrol aircraft worth $80 million and Landing Platform Docks (LPD). Despite recent momentum in Indonesia's plan to develop a major indigenous defence industry, it would take decades before Indonesia can match South Korea's current defence production capability.[82]

Indonesia's defence planners are mindful that the military build-up in the region, including its own, could have potentially destabilizing consequences. As the Defence Ministry notes:

> We should be mindful that there are indeed inherent perceptional sensitivities in military build-ups that could create miscalculation, misjudgment, and mistrust. Therefore in order to avoid military modernization currently conducted by many countries from degenerating to become a destabilizing arms race, there is a real need for strategic transparency.[83]

But Indonesia's military modernization has not yet caused anxieties in the region. This is partly due to doubts whether Jakarta can sustain a large-scale military buildup through foreign and domestic arms purchases in the near or medium term. As a defence analyst in Singapore, a country which continues to harbour fears of Indonesia, puts it, Indonesia's defence acquisition would not have "any significant implication for regional security and stability, apart from generally positive ones", thereby implying that neighbours would welcome Indonesia's increased ability to deal with non-traditional security issues such as terrorism, piracy and natural disasters.[84]

Notes

[1]   These include agreements with India in 2005, Australia in 2005, China in 2005, Japan in 2006, and the US in 2010. Indonesia has also concluded similar agreements with 12 other countries and the European Union. Agreements were signed with Russia in 2003, UK in 2006, South Korea in 2007. Note that these three countries are major arms suppliers to Indonesia. A comprehensive agreement with the EU was signed in 2009. With the exception of Russia, all the other agreements were concluded during the Yudhoyono government. Source: Indonesian Foreign Ministry.

[2]   President George W. Bush at Civil Society meeting in Bogor, 20 November 2006.

[3]   President Barack Obama's remarks at the University of Indonesia, 10 November 2010.

[4]   Hillary Rodham Clinton, remarks by Secretary of State with Indonesian Foreign Minister Hassan Wirajuda after their meeting, 8 June 2009.

[5]   Author's interview with a senior Western diplomat, 4 March 2014.

[6]   Bruce Vaughn, "Indonesia: Domestic Politics, Strategic Dynamics, and U.S. Interests", CRS Report for Congress, Washington, D.C.: Congressional Research Service, 31 January 2011 <https://www.fas.org/sgp/crs/row/RL32394.pdf>

[7]   Foreign Minister Marty Natalegawa at Banyan Tree Leadership, Forum, CSIS, 17 September 2010.

[8]   Office of the Spokesperson, U.S. Department of State, "Fact Sheet: United States-Indonesia Relations", 3 September 2012 <http://www.state.gov/r/pa/prs/ps/2012/09/197277.htm>

[9]   President Susilo Bambang Yudhoyono at the USINDO Luncheon, 14 November 2008.

[10]   Office of the Spokesperson, U.S. Department of State, "Fact Sheet: United States-Indonesia Relations", 3 September 2012 <http://www.state.gov/r/pa/prs/ps/2012/09/197277.htm>

[11]   U.S. Department of State, Office of the Spokesman, 4 January 2006 <http://news.findlaw.com/wash/s/20060105/20060105140725.html> (accessed 14 June 2008).

12 ˙Guide to U.S. Security Assistance to Indonesia and East Timor", (revised April 2008) <http://www.etan.org/news/2007/milglossary.htm.>

13 Statement of Admiral William J. Fallon, U.S. Navy Commander U.S. Pacific Command Before the Senate Armed Services Committee on the U.S. Pacific Command Posture, 8 March 2005, p. 23 <http://www.shaps.hawaii.edu/security/us/2005/20050308_fallon.html> (accessed 14 June 2008).

14 "US moves to arm Indonesia's growing F-16 fighter fleet" <http://www.reuters.com/article/2012/08/25/usa-indonesia-arms-idUSL2E8JOGMO20120825>

15 Hassan Wirajuda, interview with the author, Jakarta, 10 March 2014.

16 Vaughn, op.cit.

17 Walter Lohman, "U.S.-Indonesia Relations: Build for Endurance, Not Speed", *Backgrounder,* 4 March 2010, No. 2381. The Heritage Foundation, p. 2.

18 For background to the US role in Indonesia in the 1950s, see George McT. Kahin and Audrey R. Kahin, *Subversion as Foreign Policy: The Secret Eisenhower and Dulles Debacle in Indonesia* (New York: The New Press, 1995).

19 "Remarks by His Excellency Wen Jiabao Premier of the People's Republic of China at China-Indonesia Strategic Business Dialogue", 30 April 2011. <http://www.fmprc.gov.cn/eng/wjb/zzjg/yzs/gjlb/2716/2717/t820936.shtml>

20 Patrick Nathan, "Indonesia's Relations With China: Analyzing Strategic Reorientation, Jakarta's Motivations and Beijing's Strategic Value" <http://www.mindef.gov.sg/safti/pointer/back/journals/2001/Vol27_2/4.htm>

21 "Remarks by His Excellency Wen Jiabao Premier of the People's Republic of China At China-Indonesia Strategic Business Dialogue", 30 April 2011. <http://www.fmprc.gov.cn/eng/wjb/zzjg/yzs/gjlb/2716/2717/t820936.shtml>

22 Aris Heru Utomo, "Deepening China and Indonesia partnership", *The Jakarta Post,* 2 October 2013 <http://www.thejakartapost.com/news/2013/10/02/deepening-china-and-indonesia-partnership.html>

23 Cited in John Garnaut, "Rise of China dampens local squabbles between Australia and Indonesia", *The Age* (Melbourne), 29 April 2014 <http://www.theage.com.au/comment/rise-of-china-dampens-local-squabbles-between-australia-and-indonesia-20140429-zr191.html#ixzz30NGsxpbV>

24 Prime Minister Paul Keating during his visit in Indonesia to meet Suharto in 1994. Quoted in Bilveer Singh, *Defense Relations Between Australia and Indonesia in the Post-Cold War Era.* (Connecticut: Greenwood Publishing Group, 2002), pp. 89–93.

25 Excerpts of the speech of Prime Minister Tony Abbott titled, "Building an Indonesia-Australia Relationship for the 21st Century" on 1 October 2013, Jakarta <http://www.pm.gov.au/media/2013-10-01/building-indonesia-australia-relationship-21st-century>

26 Excerpts of the speech to the Indonesia-Australia Defence Alumni Association (IKAHAN) "IKAHAN Discussion Series – *Malam Ceramah*" on the Australia-Indonesia Defence Relationship, 3 April 2013, Jakarta <http://www.minister.defence.gov.au/2013/04/03/minister-for-defence-speech-ikhan-discussion-series-malam-ceramah-on-the-australia-indonesia-defence-relationship/>

27   Ibid.

28   Ministry of Foreign Affairs, Republic of Indonesia <http://www.kemlu.go.id/ Pages/IFPDisplay.aspx?Name=BilateralCooperation&IDP=56&P=Bilateral&l=en>

29   "Speech by the President of Indonesia before the Australian Parliament", 10 March 2010 <http://www.kemlu.go.id/Pages/SpeechTranscriptionDisplay.aspx?Name1=Pidato&Name2=Presiden&IDP=486&l=en>

30   Ibid.

31   Ibid.

32   Ibid.

33   Ibid.

34   Ibid.

35   "Operation Sovereign Borders", <http://www.customs.gov.au/site/operation-sovereign-borders.asp>

36   Review of Operation Sovereign Borders vessel positioning, December 2013 – January 2014 <http://www.customs.gov.au/webdata/resources/files/Terms_of_Reference_Review_of_Operation_Sovereign_Borders_vessel_positioning.pdf>

37   Quoted in Geraldine Nordfeldt, "Spying rocks Indonesia-Australia relations", 22 November 2013 <http://www.aljazeera.com/indepth/features/2013/11/spying-rocks-indonesia-australia-relations-2013112213361694819.html>

38   Ibid.

39   Mustaqim Adamrah, "Bilateral relations: Indonesia, Japan 'close friends' in economy, disaster", *The Jakarta Post*, 12 July 2011 <http://www.thejakartapost.com/news/2011/07/12/bilateral-relations-indonesia-japan-%E2%80%98close-friends%E2%80%99-economy-disaster.html>

40   Zheng Shibo, "News Analysis: Japan PM's visit to Indonesia to bolster economic ties between two countries", 19 January 2013 <http://news.xinhuanet.com/english/indepth/2013-01/19/c_132113755.htm>

41   Mustaqim Adamrah, op. cit.

42   Excerpt from "Indonesia and Japan – 50 Years of Partnership" by Prof. Dr. Ginandjar Kartasasmita, Chairman of the House of Regional Representatives of the Republic of Indonesia, and Chairman of Indonesia and Japan Friendship Association <http://www.id.emb-japan.go.jp/oda/en/topics_ginanjar.htm>

43   Jusuf Wanandi, "Japan-Indonesia relations: A 50 year journey", *The Jakarta Post*, 24 March 2008 <http://www.thejakartapost.com/news/2008/03/23/japanindonesia-relations-a-50-year-journey.html>

44   Ibid.

45   An excerpt of the "Opening Statements" of President Yudhoyono during the Joint Press Conference by Prime Minister Yukio Hatoyama of Japan and President Susilo Bambang Yudhoyono of Indonesia on the Occasion of the Bali Democracy

Forum II in Bali, Indonesia, 10 December 2009 <http://www.kantei.go.jp/foreign/hatoyama/statement/200912/10bali_kaiken_e.html>

[46] C. Raja Mohan, "India and Indonesia: A New Strategic Partnership", 6 February 2011 <http://www.eurasiareview.com/06022011-india-and-indonesia-a-new-strategic-partnership/>

[47] Ristian Atriandi Supriyanto, "The Unfulfilled Promise of Indonesia-India Defense Ties", 31 May 2013. <http://thediplomat.com/2013/05/the-unfulfilled-promise-of-indonesia-india-defense-ties/>

[48] Rajeev Sharma, "India, Indonesia and the China Factor", 12 October 2013. <http://www.firstpost.com/world/india-indonesia-and-the-china-factor-1168189.html>

[49] Pankaj K. Jha, "India-Indonesia: Towards Strategic Convergence", *IDSA Comment,* 24 January 2011 <http://www.idsa.in/idsacomments/IndiaIndonesiaTowardsStrategicConvergence_pkjha_240111>

[50] Sam Perlo-Freeman, Elisabeth Sköns, Carina Solmirano, and Helén Wilandh. "Trends in World Military Expenditure, 2012". (Stockholm International Peace Research Institute (SIPRI), April 2013), p. 5 <http://books.sipri.org/files/FS/SIPRIFS1304.pdf.>

[51] Ibid., p. 2.

[52] Paul Holtom, Mark Bromley, Pieter D. Wezeman and Siemon T. Wezeman."Trends in International Arms Transfers, 2012". Stockholm International Peace Research Institute, March 2013, p. 1 <http://books.sipri.org/files/FS/SIPRIFS1303.pdf>

[53] Perlo-Freeman et al., op. cit.

[54] Rizal Sukma, "Indonesia's Security Outlook, Defense Policy and Regional Cooperation", National Institute for Defense Studies, Japan, Joint Research Series 5 (October 2010) <http://www.nids.go.jp/english/publication/joint_research/series5/pdf/5-1.pdf, p. 10.>

[55] Sukma, op. cit., p. 11.

[56] Ibid., p. 12.

[57] Ministry of Defence, Indonesia, response to the author's questions, Jakarta, 16 January 2014.

[58] Benjamin Schreer, "Moving beyond ambitions? Indonesia's military modernization", Australian Strategic Policy Institute, November 2013, <https://www.aspi.org.au/publications/moving-beyond-ambitions-indonesias-military-modernisation/Strategy_Moving_beyond_ambitions.pdf>, p. 12.

[59] Ministry of Defence, Indonesia, response to the author's questions, Jakarta, 16 January 2014.

[60] Major General Dadi Susanto, Director General of Defence Strategy, "Indonesia Defence Diplomacy: Current Challenges Internal and External", Indonesian Department of Defence, May 2007 <http://www.dcaf.ch/content/download/34195/523607/version/1/file/ev_jakarta_070522susanto.pdf>

[61] Sukma, op. cit., p. 14.

[62] Ministry of Defence, Indonesia, response to the author's questions, Jakarta, 16 January 2014.

[63] "Indonesia – Armed Forces", *Jane's Sentinel Security Assessment – Southeast Asia*, 29 January 2014.

[64] Quoted in Dzirhan Mahadzir, "Indonesia's Military Modernization", *Asian Military Review*, 1 November 2012 <http://www.asianmilitaryreview.com/indonesias-military-modernization/>

[65] Ministry of Defence, Indonesia, response to the author's questions, Jakarta, 16 January 2014.

[66] The list below is developed from the following sources: Pierre Tran, "Indonesia's Big Procurement Push Is Aided By Lenders", *Defense News*, 31 March 2013, <http://www.defensenews.com/article/20130331/DEFREG03/303310002/Indonesia-8217-s-Big-Procurement-Push-Aided-By-Lenders>; "Indonesia's purchases of arms from abroad" <http://news.asiaone.com/News/AsiaOne+News/Asia/Story/A1Story20120303-331370.html#sthash.wQ2rGeSI.dpuf>; Matthias Gebauer and Otfried Nassauer, "Arms Exports: Berlin Approves Huge Tank Deal with Indonesia", *Spiegel online International*, 8 May 2013 <http://www.spiegel.de/international/germany/german-government-approves-export-of-tanks-to-indonesia-a-898698.html>; Bagus BT Saragih, "RI Central in US Rebalancing", *The Jakarta Post*, 27 August 2013 <http://m.thejakartapost.com/news/2013/08/27/ri-central-us-rebalancing.html>; Alan Warnes, "Indonesian Air Force Draws Up Shopping List", 7 February 2014 <http://www.ainonline.com/aviation-news/singapore-air-show/2014-02-07/indonesian-air-force-draws-shopping-list>

[67] Some analysts suggest that although Indonesia has signed MoUs with ROK to build these boats, whether it will able to do so is an entirely different question.

[68] Warnes, op. cit., 2014.

[69] "Indonesia Tank Deal Raises Moral Questions", *DW* (*Deutsche Welle*), 5 November 2012 <http://www.dw.de/indonesia-tank-deal-raises-moral-questions/a-16357173>.

[70] "Indonesian Navy to buy 4 Dutch corvettes", 28 October 2005 <http://english.people.com.cn/200510/28/eng20051028_217350.html>

[71] "Steel Cutting Ceremony for Indonesian Frigate", 15 Jan 2014 <http://www.damen.com/en/news/2014/01/steel-cutting-for-sigma-10514-pkr-frigate-started>

[72] "Indonesia to buy frigates from Britain", *Asian Defense*, 18 January 2013, <http://www.asian-defence.com/2013/01/indonesia-to-buy-frigates-from-britain.html?utm_source=feedburner&utm_medium=feed&utm_campaign=Feed%3A+AsianDefense+%28Asian+Defense%29>

[73] "Indonesia's Air Force Adds More Flankers", *Defense Industry Daily*, 8 January 2014 <http://www.defenseindustrydaily.com/indonesias-air-force-adds-more-flankers-03691/>

[74] Zachary Keck, "Indonesia Might Purchase Russian Su-35 Fighters", *The Diplomat*, 9 January 2014 <http://thediplomat.com/2014/01/indonesia-might-purchase-russian-su-35-fighters/>

[75] "All 16 KAI T-50s delivered to Indonesia" <http://airheadsfly.com/2014/02/22/all-16-kai-t-50s-delivered-to-indonesia/>

[76] Schreer, op. cit., p. 19. Much of the information in this paragraph is derived from this source.

[77] Ibid.

[78] Ibid.

[79] Carl Thayer, "Southeast Asian States Deploy Conventional Submarines", *The Diplomat*, 3 January 2014 <http://thediplomat.com/2014/01/southeast-asian-states-deploy-conventional-submarines/>

[80] Schreer, op. cit., p. 8.

[81] Purnomo Yusgiantoro, interview with the author, Jakarta, 16 January 2014. In a nearly two-hour briefing given to the author, the Minister, accompanied by his senior staff, explained Indonesia's maritime strategy with a focus on sea-lanes security which he also presented as a public good.

[82] Trefor Moss, "No alarm bells over Jakarta's military drive", *Asia Times*, 5 November 2010 <http://www.atimes.com/atimes/Southeast_Asia/LK05Ae01.html>

[83] Ministry of Defence, Indonesia, response to the author's questions, Jakarta, 16 January 2014.

[84] Moss, op. cit.,

Chapter 5

INDONESIA AS A
GLOBAL ACTOR

The Strategic Plan (2005–25) of Indonesia's Foreign Ministry (Rencana Strategis Kementerian Luar Negeri) makes many references to the country's global role. As the document puts it, the goal of Indonesian foreign policy is to "increase the role of Indonesia as a leader and its contribution to international cooperation" and "increase Indonesia's diplomatic role in handling multilateral issues". This is not pure idealism. Multilateral diplomacy is "a means to safeguard national security, territorial integrity, and the protection of natural resources". In the past, active participation in instruments of international law, such as the United Nations Convention on the Law of the Sea (UNCLOS), has enabled Indonesia to secure its national interest as an archipelagic state by gaining greater control over its maritime resources. Such considerations remain important, hence the call to "optimize diplomacy through implementation on international laws and international cooperation in order to protect national interest". But a globalist orientation is also geared to enhancing "Indonesia's image in the world".[1]

Of course it is not new for Indonesia to engage itself in global diplomacy. During the Suharto era, it played an active role in forums of the developing countries such as the Non-Aligned Movement (NAM) and in North-South negotiations. But there are major shifts. One is to project its democratic credentials on the world stage – something that the authoritarian regime of Suharto could not do. In a world increasingly conscious of the importance of the protection of the environment and cultural assets, Indonesia as a country with vast environmental resources and a rich cultural heritage, is also mindful of paying attention to these. Hence, the goal of the global diplomacy of new Indonesia is to be "accepted" by the international community "as a country that highly regards its human rights and pays attention to environmental issues and [promotes] an international regime that upholds and respects Indonesia's cultural heritage". Another shift is in the arena of economic and development diplomacy. Whereas Indonesia was and remains part of the Group of 77 (G-77) of developing countries, its membership in the relatively new G-20 – a far more limited grouping comprising both developed and developing countries – provides it the opportunity to craft a new image and role in the international arena.

The UN remains a focus of Indonesia's multilateral diplomacy. Thus, increasing its role in safeguarding security and world peace requires "active participation in contributing ideas and thoughts in UN resolutions and declarations". Like many emerging powers, it also pays particular attention to the reform of the UN system, which is particularly seen in its "active participation in pushing for the reformation of the UN Security Council". It was elected as a non-permanent member of the UN Security Council (UNSC) in 2006. Further, it served as one of the four vice-presidents of the UN Human Rights Council during its fourth cycle (2009–10).

While Indonesia's global engagement is varied and multifaceted, of particular importance are its engagement with relatively new institutions, such as the G-20, and in promoting new norms such as the Responsibility to Protect (R2P).

G-20

One of the most important aspects of Indonesia's new profile in global governance is its membership in the G-20. Originally established in 1999 in response to the 1997 Asian financial crisis, the G-20 was upgraded to a summit level conclave of established and emerging nations in 2008 to manage the unfolding global financial crisis. According to Mahendra Siregar, Chairman, Indonesia Investment Coordinating Board (BKPM), and the G-20 "Sherpa" for Indonesia, Indonesia was not surprised to be invited to the G-20 summit because it was already invited to the ministerial level at the very outset.[2] But for Indonesia, the G-20's importance goes well beyond financial crisis management. Siregar says that the G-20 is "not just about financial crisis, but also about new ideas on more balanced, sustainable and inclusive growth. That is the emphasis of Indonesia and developing countries."[3]

Indonesia views the G-20 as a major platform for its global role. According to Foreign Minister Marty Natalegawa, "The G-20, which is a group with limited members and with Indonesia as a permanent member, can be used to present Indonesia as an influential player on the global level."[4] Membership in the G-20 brings important opportunities and benefits. Indonesia's economic position is changing from that of being a low-income country to a middle-income country and from being an aid beneficiary to both a beneficiary and a donor country. These changes require updating its "profile in the outside world". An active role in the G-20 serves this end, for the G-20 can serve as an "external political instrument for Indonesia's progress towards becoming a developed country". Moreover, Indonesia views the G-20 as a medium through which it can share its experiences and "success stories" in development.[5]

Indonesia's agenda and role in the G-20 can be described as comprising a representative agenda, a development agenda, and what it calls a "civilization bridge-builder" role. On the first, Indonesia aims to represent not just ASEAN but the whole developing world, with particular emphasis on their needs. Indonesia successfully pushed hard for ASEAN to be invited to be an observer to the G-20. As the presidential spokesperson (later Indonesia's ambassador to the US) Dino Patti Djalal put it in 2010: "Indonesia will...underline the importance of preserving worldwide economic resilience, particularly when it comes to developing countries, which are very prone to financial crises..."[6] As an example of this role, Indonesia would support the creation of a global financial safety net to complement the International Monetary Fund (IMF) and the World Bank. The Indonesian Foreign Ministry claims that "Indonesia's role in each G-20 Summit has always been to promote the interests of developing countries and to maintain an inclusive and sustainable global economic system". Such initiatives include its proposal to establish a global expenditure support fund, as well as efforts to prevent premature discontinuation of fiscal stimulus packages in advanced countries which could harm the developing countries.[7]

Indonesia has also pushed development issues within the G-20, with a strong priority to infrastructure development, and the reform of international financial institutions. "Indonesia is very much involved," according to Siregar, in the deliberations over both issues within G-20 meetings. It worked with France on the reform of international financial institutions that led to agreement on increased voting weightage for emerging economies, and an increase in IMF capitalization.[8] Indonesia's agenda also focuses on placing financial inclusion, social safety nets and aid for trade and food security on the G-20 agenda.[9]

Indonesia has championed the development of micro-finance in its push for innovative financial inclusion on the basis of a strong regulatory framework that must also pay due regard to international standards and national circumstances.[10]

While the G-20's work is mainly that of an economic forum (it claims to be the "world's premier forum for international economic cooperation"[10]), Indonesia finds in it a broader significance. The third agenda has to do with the opportunity to "play the self-perceived role as a bridge-builder between diverse civilizations".[11] President Yudhoyono once described the G-20 as

> …one manifestation of the change taking place in global politics. The G-20 grouping, comprising some 85 per cent of the world's GNP and 80 per cent of world trade, is not just an economic powerhouse – it is also a civilizational powerhouse. The G-20 for the first time accommodates all the major civilizations – not just Western countries, but also China, South Korea, India, South Africa, and others, including significantly, three countries with large Muslim populations: Saudi Arabia, Turkey, and Indonesia. The G-7, the G-8, or even the United Nations Security Council, does not boast this distinction. The G-20 is representative of a multi-civilizational global community.[12]

Indonesia's key initiatives in the G-20 include being an initiator of the General Expenditure Support Fund (GESF) and co-chairing of working groups. The GESF is aimed at providing liquidity of funding from the IMF and the World Bank to help support developing countries during a crisis especially in meeting their needs in developing infrastructure, creating jobs and financing Millennium Development Goals (MDGs) programmes.[13] Indonesia co-chaired, together with France, a G-20 working group whose main purpose was studying multilateral development banks in order to improve their management and development impact. Indonesia has called for diversifying the sources of their funding, providing recommendations to developing countries to overcome development policy constraints, involving the private sector and developing well-advised projects priorities.[14] Indonesia has also co-chaired the G-20's Anti-Corruption Working Group, whose task includes preparing strategies to curb corruption as a major challenge to national development.[15]

As part of its role in the G-20, Indonesia also seeks to inject a greater sense of equality in the grouping. The G-20 is "not the most open, democratic process, but [is] crisis-driven," says Siregar.[16] Indonesia is mindful of the limitations of the G-20 which is often viewed by its critics as a selective financial cartel of nations which, despite comprising countries of both the North and the South, is still dominated inside by the North. Hence Indonesia's goal would be to keep the G-20 as "a democratic forum in which all of its members have the opportunity of speaking on equal footing with any country" and to prevent it from being manipulated by "any dominating pressure or stringent attitude/ position from the G-20 member states".[17] Siregar believes that progress on that score is being made, observing that previously "Western interest dominated the G-20, [now there is a] broader interest."[18]

It is premature to conclude the success of Indonesia's role within the G-20, especially at a time when the relevance of the grouping is itself uncertain. Indonesia itself is realistic about the prospects for the grouping: "unless it improves its accountability and role in global finance and economic issues, the relevance of the G-20 will be questioned".[19] There have been criticisms that Jakarta does not pull its weight within the group. Despite its obvious interest in and enthusiasm for the G-20, Indonesia maintains a "low profile" in the grouping, in keeping with the "traditional Indonesian approach". As Sinegar puts it: Indonesia "does not want to be dominant, [it's] not our culture".[20] Moreover, the G-20 comprises nations much more powerful than Indonesia, a structural constraint that would limit how much Indonesia can accomplish within the group.

Although Indonesia sees a broader role for the G-20, it does not believe that the G-20 should tackle political and security issues. Siregar says that while the G-20 can be used to address other issues, promote reform in other forums such as the WTO, and tackle climate change, it should focus on finance and other economic issues such as development. As he puts it "although you cannot afford not to discuss other issues", it is best not to deal with "totally new political security issues but [only] those with relevance to economic and financial issues". In his view, the G-20 already has a crowded agenda. And there are other forums to discuss other issues such as climate change.[21]

Responsibility to Protect

The Responsibility to Protect (R2P) doctrine stipulates the state's responsibility to protect its population from genocide, war crimes, ethnic cleansing, and crimes against humanity; the international community's responsibility to help states exercise their responsibility to protect; and – most critically and controversially – the international community's readiness to intervene (through economic sanctions or, as a last resort, military intervention) when a state shows it cannot or will not exercise its responsibility to protect. Like many developing countries, Indonesia has had some concerns about the R2P. As former Foreign Minister Hassan Wirajuda told this author: the R2P is a "continuation or extension of an approach of the West which tends to politicize human rights". Sometimes, this approach means "less dialogue". As he puts it, "We in the developing world rejected humanitarian intervention" because of key questions such as: "Who mandates, who judges".[22]

Officially Indonesia has lent support to the doctrine, however. At the 2005 UN World Summit, it pledged to adopt the R2P doctrine. To support the principle is to act in line with Indonesia's current foreign policy priorities, such as the support of democratization, rule of law, and human rights in its neighbourhood. R2P also provides it with the framework to play a greater role in promoting change in Myanmar and the justification to build a stronger, more active ASEAN.

A clear official exposition of Indonesia's position on the R2P came in 2009, when Natalegawa, then the Permanent Representative to the UN, said: "...the task ahead is not to reinterpret or renegotiate the conclusions of the World Summit [affirming the R2P], rather to find ways of implementing its decisions." He stated that while Indonesia supported the R2P norm, more emphasis should be given to non-military options:

> We are not in disagreement with the three pillars of the responsibility to protect, namely: the primary responsibility of every state to protect its population from genocide, war crimes, ethnic cleansing and crimes against humanity; the responsibility of the international community to assist States to fulfill their national obligations, including capacity-building; and the commitment to take timely and decisive action, consistent with the UN Charter, in those situations where a state is manifestly failing in its responsibility to protect...It is worth to emphasize, however, that pillar three also encompasses a wide-range of non-coercive and non-violent response under Chapter VI and VIII of the Charter.

Natalegawa called for more emphasis on prevention measures and to the strengthening of capacity-building programmes. He warned, "It is important not to underestimate the magnitude of the challenge ahead in operationalizing the concept."[23]

Indonesia was not yet a non-permanent member of the UNSC when it authorized the use of force against the Gaddafi regime in Libya in 2011. But Indonesia's response was cautious. – Natalegawa called for a ceasefire and an end to airstrikes on 28 March 2011 and said his government condemned violence on all sides.[24] On 5 April, President Susilo Bambang Yudhoyono said that after a ceasefire was agreed, Indonesia would gladly contribute to a UN peacekeeping effort in the war-torn Libya.[25]

The Non-Aligned Movement (NAM)

Despite the end of the Cold War, and general improvement in North-South relations, reflected not least in Indonesia's membership in the G-20, Jakarta continues to emphasize the importance of the Non-Aligned Movement (NAM). It prides itself as being one of the founders of NAM, its genesis in the Asian African Conference held in Bandung in 1955, and highlights NAM's "crucial role in Indonesia's foreign policy". Committed to the continuing relevance of NAM, it also played a "vital role in the efforts of increasing the role of NAM to encourage peace, international security, dialogue, and cooperation in attempts to address intra and inter conflict through peaceful resolution and efforts in tackling new global issues."[26] Speaking at the Commemorative Meeting of the 50th Anniversary of NAM hosted by Indonesia in Bali on 25 May 2011, President Yudhoyono stated:

> Today, we celebrate half a century of our Movement's long struggle for a better world. As a founding member of the Non-Aligned, Indonesia is honored and humbled to be part of this largest movement for peace in history. As we mark our achievements, this is also a good time for all of us, to determine how the Non-Aligned can be a greater force for peace, justice and prosperity in the 21st century.[27]

It should be recalled that Indonesia was the chair of NAM from 1992 to 1995. In the official Indonesian view, NAM, now a grouping of 120 nations, can "contribute significantly at the United Nations and other international forums in developing adequate and sustainable responses to issues pertaining to peace and security, development, human rights, democracy, disarmament, terrorism, and gender equality and empowerment".[28] It can be "proactive" in helping "shape the world" in the 21st century, with a "new vision and approach."[29] Indonesia has used NAM as a platform for voicing its position on a range of global issues, such as debates on conventional weapons (e.g., small arms and light weapons), nuclear weapons, the disarmament-development nexus, and the Palestine issue, among others. Indonesia also represented the NAM States Parties to the Treaty on the Non-Proliferation of Nuclear Weapons at its Review Conference in May 2010 and restated one of the group core demands: complete nuclear disarmament.[30] NAM has also served as an important forum to pursue Indonesia's goal of creating a sovereign Palestinian state and eventually making Palestine a full member of the UN (the Indonesian Government has had official diplomatic relations with the Palestinian Authority since October 1989).

The Organization of Islamic Conference (OIC)

Another global platform for Indonesia's voice is the Organization of Islamic Conference (OIC), which represents over 1.5 billion Muslims and the second largest intergovernmental organization after the United Nations. Indonesia has sought the "revitalization" of the OIC. "As the country with the largest Moslem (sic) population Indonesia has a responsibility to support the OIC to encourage good governance in the Islamic community and to promote OIC as a credible, competent international organization."[31] The OIC serves as a vehicle for advancing Indonesia's international goals, such as the creation of an independent Palestinian state. It is also useful for promoting Indonesia's Islamic credentials, while at the same time promoting its democratic vision of Islam. Indonesia has supported the idea of a global ban on blasphemy at the UN. In September 2012, President Yudhoyono, in his address to the UN General Assembly, supported the idea (a similar call was made by then Pakistani President Asif Ali Zardari) for a "legally binding, global anti-blasphemy protocol", referring to the film, *The Innocence of Muslims*. Arguing that insulting the Prophet Mohammed is illegitimate free speech and violence-inducing, he noted, "Freedom of expression is therefore not absolute."[32] At the same time, Indonesia played a major role in the creation of the OIC's Independent Permanent Human Rights Commission (IPHRC) in 2011 and hosted its first meeting in February 2012, a move that attested to its desire to encourage and support a moderate, democratic brand of Islam. President Yudhoyono has called for an "Islamic Renaissance" through "a peaceful and constructive 'jihad' through the newly-revised OIC charter promoting democracy and human rights.[33] The OIC has proved a practical vehicle for Indonesia's role as a facilitator and mediator, especially in the conflict between the Philippine Government and the separatist group, the Moro National Liberation Front (MNLF). Indonesia serves as the chair of the OIC Peace Committee for the Southern Philippines (OIC-PCSP), which held Tripartite Meetings to further the peace process in the Southern Philippines and achieve peaceful conflict resolution.

Climate Change

Indonesia's policy towards climate change stems from national security concerns: as a large nation with over 13,000 islands which could be threatened by rising sea levels, as well as a country with one of the largest rainforest covers which are threatened by commercial activities and expanding population. Another concern is the impact of climate change in lowering crop yields – especially important for a nation whose economy is still substantially agricultural.[34] When it comes to environmental issues, Indonesia has received both praise and criticism. In a speech in Indonesia in November 2011, UN-Secretary General Ban Ki-moon called Indonesia a "world leader on combating deforestation".[35] Despite this positive perception, Indonesia has been blamed for not controlling the forest fires that have caused haze over large parts of Southeast Asia, including neighbouring Singapore and Malaysia.

Indonesia has sought to burnish its credentials in international fora as a leader in the fight against climate change. President Yudhoyono was the lead speaker on climate change issues at the G-20 summit in 2009 in Pittsburg.[36] Before that, it played host to the UN Conference on Climate Change in Bali in 2007.[37] Indonesia has backed up the "common but differentiated responsibility" (CBDR) norm (which Yudhoyono called "common and shared responsibility".) As he put it "...in the spirit of this partnership, I believe that developed countries must take the lead in reducing their greenhouse gas emissions, while developing countries must do more. This is what I call common and shared responsibility."[38]

Indonesia has been a strong supporter of the global initiative, Reducing Emissions from Deforestation and Forest Degradation (REDD), which aims to create a financial value for the carbon stored in forests. A notable initiative is the Indonesian Task Force for Reducing Emissions from Deforestation and Forest Degradation (REDD+), in partnership with the Government of Norway, whose aim is to improve forest and peatland governance. The UN opened its first Office for REDD+ Coordination in Indonesia (UNORCID)."[39]

In 2009, Indonesia committed itself to reducing the country's greenhouse gas emissions by 26 per cent by 2020, using domestic resources and 41 per cent with international support. It has launched One Billion Indonesia Trees for the World (OBIT) programme. It has a 2011 moratorium on the issuance of new forest and peatland licences, now extended for another two years. The Indonesian Constitutional Court has decided that customary forest, or *hutanadat*, is not part of the state forest zone, thereby recognizing the land and resources rights of *adat* community and forest-dependent communities.

Reform of Global Institutions

As noted, Indonesia along with other emerging powers, has championed the need for reform of global institutions. In his remarks in the UN General Assembly on 25 September 2012, President Yudhoyono lamented on the "outdated international security architecture" of the UN Security Council (UNSC).[40] Vice-President Boediono has pointed to the ineffectiveness of the UNSC in brokering agreement between conflicting factions in the Syrian conflict.[41] Yudhoyono compared the UNSC with the G-20 Summit, saying that the latter has been "more representative of today's global dynamics" than the former, which "still reflects the power balance of 1945 rather than 2009". For Indonesia, "this situation is unsustainable. The UN Security Council will need to be restructured to keep up with 21st century geopolitical realities."[42] Jakarta also sees a link between its own democratization and its championing of global governance reform. "Critical to our democratic work at the global level is global governance. It is a governance that fully subscribes to democratic principles. It is a governance that strengthens international peace and security, advances economic development and promotes effective enjoyment of human rights."[43] But reform should not stop at the UN, though; rather it should extend to other groups, including international bodies such as the World Bank, IMF, OIC and OPEC, as well as regional ones like NATO, APEC and ASEAN. And reform should be comprehensive, covering both the economic and security fields.[44]

Indonesia is realistic about how far the reform of the UN can proceed and what role it can play in influencing the debates over the nature of that reform. In 1999, Ambassador Makarim Wibisono, its Permanent Representative to the UN while speaking on behalf of NAM, admitted that the UNSC reform is "one of the most difficult issues ever faced by member states of our Organization".[45] Former Foreign Minister Hassan Wirajuda is not optimistic of the UNSC reform, either. He asks: "How can one change the privilege of P5?" He argues that it would take a major crisis to move the process of UN reform forward.[46]

Indonesia is not an aspirant to a permanent membership in the UNSC. There are two other Asian contenders – Japan and India – which would certainly take precedence over Indonesia should there be agreement over expanding the permanent membership. (It is noteworthy that in 2006, President Yudhoyono "expressed Indonesia's support for Japan's permanent membership in the Council".[47]) But there are other scenarios under which Indonesia may get to play a more important role in the UN decision-making. For example, if there is a dilution of the veto system (such as double veto rule), it will give holders of non-permanent seats (which would be open to Indonesia from time to time) more clout. Representation of regional groups could also make Indonesia – as leader of ASEAN – influence the UNSC decision-making indirectly. However, none of the proposals currently being tabled has any realistic chance of being adopted due to the resistance of the existing permanent five (P5) members to relinquish their special privileges.

In the absence of any realistic prospects for any structural reform of the UNSC, Indonesia has supported other pathways to reform such as improving its "working mechanism and transparency".[48] It has also supported giving greater authority to the UN General Assembly to override the veto. Thus, in the General Assembly, "the NAM's numerical superiority can be put to work, in the cause of peace and development".[49] President Yudhoyono calls for "a harmony between the aspirations of the Security Council Members and members of the General Assembly. Such harmony requires the promotion of multilateralism and rejection of unilateralism…"[50] Moreover, it has supported giving "a bigger role to regional organizations in the global decision-making process, because they were in a better position to understand and assess the root causes and particularities of the multi-dimensional challenges that had arisen from their respective regions".[51]

Bali Democracy Forum

Although regional in scope, the Bali Democracy Forum (BDF) further reflects Indonesia's global aspirations as promoter of democracy. In December 2008, Indonesia launched this regional initiative. Known as the brainchild of President Yudhoyono and strongly backed by then Foreign Minister Hassan Wirajuda, the BDF is an annual intergovernmental forum.[52]

Each annual meeting of the BDF has a thematic focus. The theme of BDF I in 2008 was "Building Democracy and Consolidating Democracy: A Strategic Agenda for Asia"; that of BDF II in 2009 was "Promoting Synergy Between Democracy, Development and Rule of Law in Asia: Prospects for Regional Cooperation"; and for BDF III in 2010 it was "Democracy and the Promotion of Peace". BDF IV in 2011 focused on "Enhancing Democratic Participation in a Changing World: Responding to Democratic Voices"; BDF V in 2012 on "Advancing Democratic Principles at the Global Setting", and BDF VI in 2013 on "Consolidating Democracy in a Pluralistic Society".[53]

Significantly, membership in the Forum is not restricted to democratic countries alone. Indonesia has made it clear that it will not pursue an aggressive posture of democracy promotion and will not close the door to countries which are not democratic or fully democratic, such as Brunei, Myanmar and China. All of them were represented at the inaugural forum. The Forum is to share ideas about democracy and develop mechanisms for mutual assistance in building democratic institutions. According to President Yudhoyono, "Indonesia should not pressure other ASEAN members to follow our path to be democratic, but by providing itself as the example, we could achieve democracy and development in the region."[54] Hassan Wirajuda, a key architect of the BDF, elaborated:

> Discussions during the Forum are aimed at promoting the sharing of experiences and best practices in promotions of democracy. There is no attempt to impose any extraneous value or to recommend a single model of democracy. To maintain a level of comfort for all, the Forum makes no judgments on the situation or conditions in any country.[55]

Highlighting that 83 countries and international organizations attended the Forum in 2013, Wirajuda has no hesitation calling it the "global premier forum of dialogue on democracy".[56] Ketut Erawan, Executive Director of the Institute of Peace and Democracy (IPD) at Udayan University in Bali, which is the implementing agency for the agenda of the BDF, describes the Forum's approach to democracy promotion as one of "sharing experiences, learning lessons".[57] Wirajuda adds that the Forum not only enables Indonesia to share its democratic experience with others but also to "learn from other democracies in order to consolidate our democratic gains".[58] The programmes undertaken by IPD are aimed at sharing experiences, knowledge and skills building, promoting democratic institutions and the rule of law, and fostering "democracy that delivers" or the "manifestation of democracy in a practical way, such as anti-corruption".[59] The BDF is a "learning community" that provides an "agenda of discourse". As an example, he cites an exchange between a Chinese delegate and the Indonesian hosts. When the former asked: "Why does Indonesia need democracy", the Indonesian replied, "Only democracy can sustain Indonesia."[60]

How do the BDF and IPD support Indonesian foreign policy? They do it in two ways. The first is by helping develop concrete programmes for Indonesia's democratic support, as with Egypt and Myanmar. The IPD has also worked with Tunisia in helping develop its new constitution, help with public diplomacy and training of diplomats. Secondly, the existence of BDF and the IPD help reorient and structure the internal policy-making processes in Indonesia in order to make it better organized and suited for democracy promotion, as well as provide more energy and incentive to promote democracy. The IPD has provided training for numerous countries including Iraq, Afghanistan, Tunisia, Egypt, Myanmar and Fiji on issues ranging from empowerment of women, drafting of constitutions, parliamentary reform, and electoral reform.[61]

According to Erawan, the regional response to the BDF has been positive because it provides a "non-threatening learning environment".[62] An Indonesian analyst supports this by saying that: "When it was first established in 2008, many may have questioned the idea of a democracy forum involving some of the least-likely 'democracies' in the region. However, when observing recent developments in Myanmar as well as other subtle democratic changes unfolding across the region, it is difficult to argue that BDF has merely been a 'talk-shop.'"[63]

But there are limitations on BDF's role. As an intergovernmental forum, the BDF is perceived to be too state-centric. One of the challenges therefore is to expand its dialogue with important stakeholders such as civil society groups (it should be noted that the IPD does take NGOs on its foreign missions). Also, the BDF needs to make a transition from being an Indonesian initiative to having an international and regional co-ownership. Further, there is the uncertainty about how the BDF will fare after Yudhoyono's presidency, since it was his brainchild. Will it receive high level support from the next president?

UN Peacekeeping

Indonesia has been one of the world's most active contributors to UN peacekeeping missions, having participated in 24 peacekeeping operations (PKOs), from 1957 to 2009. In 2013, Indonesia was participating in six UN peacekeeping missions, ranking as the world's 16th largest contributor , with 1,815 personnel deployed. The figure is likely to increase. In August 2013, Major General Imam Edy Mulyono of the TNI, a former commander of the Indonesian Defence Forces Peacekeeping Centre, was appointed Force Commander of the United Nations Mission for the Referendum in Western Sahara (MINURSO).[64] In December 2011, Indonesia announced the opening of a peacekeeping facility as part of the Indonesian Peace and Security Center in Sentul, Bogor.[65]

Rizal Sukma, Executive Director of the Centre for Strategic and International Studies (CSIS), Jakarta, points to several benefits – both domestic and external – of Indonesia's participation in UN Peace Keeping Operations (UNPKOs). In his view, participation "would contribute positively to the efforts of maintaining and preserving global security and stability" and "improve Indonesia's image abroad as a responsible member of international community". As such, peacekeeping complements Indonesia's foreign policy as it provides another avenue for engagement with the larger international community, especially those nations also active in UN peacekeeping missions and those in the conflict areas. He also argues that PKO experiences provide Indonesia with useful insights on conflict resolution and help the professionalization of the Indonesian military. The training and familiarity with tactical and combat capabilities that peacekeepers receive help the Indonesian military prepare for future missions, including domestic ones.[66]

Notes

1   Rencana Strategis Kementerian Luar Negeri (Strategic Plan of the Ministry of Foreign Affairs), (Jakarta: Kementerian Luar Negeri, 2013).

2   Mahendra Siregar, interview with the author, Jakarta, 10 March 2014.

3   Ibid.

4   Quoted in Yulius Hermawan et al. *G-20 Research Project: The Role of Indonesia in the G-20: Background, Role and Objectives of Indonesia's Membership* (Jakarta: Friedrich Ebert Stiftung Indonesia Office, 2011), p. 37.

5   Indonesia's Ministry of Foreign Affairs <http://kemlu.go.id/Pages/IFPDisplay.aspx?Name=MultilateralCooperation&IDP=11&P=Multilateral&l=en>

6   Quoted in "Indonesian president to fight for developing countries' needs at G20", *Xinhua*, 24 June 2010 <http://english.peopledaily.com.cn/90001/90777/90851/7038988.html>

7   Indonesia's Ministry of Foreign Affairs <http://kemlu.go.id/Pages/IFPDisplay.aspx?Name=MultilateralCooperation&IDP=11&P=Multilateral&l=en>

8   Mahendra Siregar, interview with the author, Jakarta, 10 March 2014.

9   President Yudhoyono's speech at Davos, 27 June 2011 <http://zh-cn.facebook.com/note.php?note_id=10150128775989747&comments&ref=mf http://www.kemlu.go.id/mexicocity/Pages/Speech.aspx?IDP=2&l=id>

10 President Yudhoyono's keynote address at the 2010 AFI Global Policy Forum in Bali, 27 September 2010 <http://www.afi-global.org/sites/default/files/keynoteadd_2010.pdf>

11 Yulius Hermawan, op. cit.

12 President Yudhoyono's speech at the Kennedy School of Government, Harvard University, 29 September 2009 <http://myquran.org/forum/showthread.php/60742-%E2%80%9CTOWARDS-HARMONY-AMONG-CIVILIZATIONS%E2%80%9D-SPEECH-BY-DR-SUSILO-BAMBANG-YUDHOYONO>

13 Yulius Hermawan, op. cit. p. 45.

14 President Yudhoyono's speech at the B20 conversations with government leaders in Selasa, 19 June 2012 <http://www.kemlu.go.id/mexicocity/Pages/Speech.aspx?IDP=2&l=id>

15 Focus Group Discussion and Workshop, "G-20 and development Agenda: Formulating Recommendations for g20 Summit in Seoul, Korea", Jakarta, Indonesia, 4 November 2010 <http://www.fes.or.id/fes/download/G20%20and%20Development.pdf>

16 Mahendra Siregar, interview with the author, Jakarta, 10 March 2014.

17 Indonesia's Ministry of Foreign Affairs <http://kemlu.go.id/Pages/IFPDisplay.aspx?Name=MultilateralCooperation&IDP=11&P=Multilateral&l=en>

18   Mahendra Siregar, op. cit.

19   Ibid.

20   Ibid.

21   Ibid.

22   Hassan Wirajuda, interview with the author, Jakarta, 12 March 2014.

23   Statement by H.E. Dr R.M. Marty M. Natalegawa, Ambassador, Permanent Representative of the Republic of Indonesia to the United Nations, New York, 23 July 2009 <http://responsibilitytoprotect.org/Indonesia_ENG_23_july.pdf>

24   "Indonesia urges ceasefire in Libya", The Jakarta Post, 28 March 2011 <http://www.thejakartapost.com/news/2011/03/28/ri-urges-ceasefire-libya.html>

25   "Turkey, Indonesia Call for Ceasefire in Libya", The Jakarta Globe, 5 April 2011 <http://www.thejakartaglobe.com/archive/turkey-indonesia-call-for-ceasefire-in-libya/>

26   Indonesia's Ministry of Foreign Affairs <http://kemlu.go.id/Pages/IFPDisplay.aspx?Name=MultilateralCooperation&IDP=3&P=Multilateral&l=en>

27   President's Yudhoyono's Inaugural Address at the Opening Session of the 16th Ministerial Conference and Commemorative Meeting of the 50th Anniversary of the Non-Aligned Movement, Bali, Indonesia, 25 May 2011 <http://www.setkab.go.id/berita-1836-fighting-for-peace-justice-and-prosperity-in-the-21st-century.html>

28   XVI Ministerial Conference and Commemorative Meeting of the Non-Aligned Movement, Bali, Indonesia, 23–27 May 2011 <http://nam.gov.ir/Portal/File/ShowFile.aspx?ID=9f5b3b6f-3416-4d9c-ae30-853af7bfeff7>

29   President's Yudhoyono's Inaugural Address at the Opening Session of the 16th Ministerial Conference and Commemorative Meeting of the 50th Anniversary of the Non-Aligned Movement, Bali, Indonesia, 25 May 2011 <http://www.setkab.go.id/berita-1836-fighting-for-peace-justice-and-prosperity-in-the-21st-century.html>

30   Statement by H.E. Dr R.M. Marty M. Natalegawa, Minister for Foreign Affairs of the Republic of Indonesia, on behalf of the NAM States Parties to the Treaty on the Non-Proliferation of Nuclear Weapons at the 2010 Review Conference of the Parties to the Treaty on the Non-Proliferation of Nuclear Weapons (NPT), New York, 3 May 2010. <http://www.indonesiamission-ny.org/menu_kiri/k1_peace_security/k1_statements/050310a.html>

31   Indonesia's Ministry of Foreign Affairs <http://www.kemlu.go.id/Pages/IFPDisplay.aspx?Name=MultilateralCooperation&IDP=4&P=Multilateral&l=en>

32   Quoted in Patrick Goodenough, "Muslim Leaders Make Case for Global Blasphemy Ban at U.N", CNSNews.com, 26 September 2012 <http://cnsnews.com/news/article/muslim-leaders-make-case-global-blasphemy-ban-un>

33 Quoted in "Muslim nations seek change, new 'Renaissance'", 15 March 2008 <http://www.middle-east-online.com/english/?id=24846>

34 President Yudhoyono's speech titled, "MANIFESTO 2015 Sustainable Growth With Equity" delivered at the Center for International Forestry Research (CIFOR) Bogor, 13 June 2012 <http://www.setkab.go.id/berita-4719-manifesto-2015-sustainable-growth-with-equity-by-dr-susilo-bambang-yudhoyono-president-of-the-republic-of-indonesia-at-the-center-for-international-forestry-research-cifor-bogor-13-june-2012.html>

35 UN Secretary-General Ban Ki-moon's opening remarks at a press conference, Palangkaraya (Indonesia), 17 November 2011 <https://www.un.org/apps/news/infocus/sgspeeches/statments_full.asp?statID=1385#.U0nl4aKy_IU>

36 Quoted in Adianto P. Simamora, "Yudhoyono to address G20 on climate change issues", *The Jakarta Post*, 24 September 2009 <http://www.thejakartapost.com/news/2009/09/24/yudhoyono-address-g20-climate-change-issues.html>

37 President Yudhoyono's Speech titled, "Indonesia's role as a regional and global actor", Annual Address of Wilton Park at the Foreign and Commonwealth Office, London, 2 November 2012 <https://www.wiltonpark.org.uk/president-yudhoyonos-speech-at-our-annual-address/>

38 President Yudhoyono's speech at the Opening of International Workshop on "Tropical Forest Alliance 2020: Promoting Sustainability and Productivity in the Palm Oil and Pulp and Paper Sectors", Jakarta, 27 June 2013 <http://www.presidenri.go.id/index.php/eng/pidato/2013/06/27/2136.html>

39 UN Secretary-General Ban Ki-moon, 17 November 2011.

40 Quoted in "Indonesia calls for reform of UN Security Council", *Antara News*, 26 September 2012 <http://www.antaranews.com/en/news/84723/indonesia-calls-for-reform-of-un-security-council>

41 Quoted in "NAM Must Contribute to World Peace: VP", *Antara News*, 31 August 2012 <http://www.embassyofindonesia.org/news/2012/08/news127.htm>

42 President Yudhoyono's speech at the Kennedy School of Government, Harvard University, 29 September 2009 <http://myquran.org/forum/showthread.php/60742-%E2%80%9CTOWARDS-HARMONY-AMONG-CIVILIZATIONS%E2%80%9D-SPEECH-BY-DR-SUSILO-BAMBANG-YUDHOYONO>

43 Quoted in Arientha Primanita, "SBY Reiterates Urgency for UN Security Council Reform", *Jakarta Globe*, 8 November 2012 <http://www.thejakartaglobe.com/archive/sby-reiterates-urgency-for-un-security-council-reform/>

44 President's Yudhoyono's Inaugural Address at the Opening Session of the 16th Ministerial Conference and Commemorative Meeting of the 50th Anniversary of the Non-Aligned Movement, Bali, Indonesia, 25 May 2011 <http://www.setkab.go.id/berita-1836-fighting-for-peace-justice-and-prosperity-in-the-21st-century.html>

45 Statement by Ambassador Makarim Wibisono, Permanent Representative of the Republic of Indonesia, in the "General Assembly Plenary Meeting on Agenda Item 38: The question of equitable representation on and increase of the membership

of the Security Council and related matters", 16 December 1999 <http://www.globalpolicy.org/component/content/article/200/32850.html>

[46] Hassan Wirajuda, interview with the author, Jakarta, 12 March 2014.

[47] Japan-Indonesia Joint Statement, "Strategic Partnership for Peaceful and Prosperous Future", November 2006 <http://www.mofa.go.jp/region/asia-paci/indonesia/joint0611.html>

[48] President Yudhoyono's speech at the Inaugural Ceremony of the 14th Annual Meeting of the Asia Pacific Parliamentary Forum (APPF) Jakarta, 16 January 2006 <http://kemlu.go.id/Pages/SpeechTranscriptionDisplay.aspx?Name1=Pidato&Name2=Presiden&IDP=253&l=en>

[49] President's Yudhoyono's Inaugural Address at the Opening Session of the 16th Ministerial Conference and Commemorative Meeting of the 50th Anniversary of the Non-Aligned Movement, Bali, Indonesia, 25 May 2011 <http://www.setkab.go.id/berita-1836-fighting-for-peace-justice-and-prosperity-in-the-21st-century.html>

[50] Arientha Primanita, op. cit.

[51] "Chair's Statement of the Fifth Bali Democracy Forum", Nusa Dua, Bali, 8–9 November 2012 <http://www.ipd.or.id/wp-content/uploads/2013/09/Chairman-Statement-of-BDF-V.pdf>

[52] The Forum begins with a leaders' session, attended by those heads of states/governments attending. One of them serves as Co-Chair of the Forum along with the President of Indonesia. Other discussions are at the ministerial level. The BDF falls under the purview of the Indonesian Foreign Ministry.

[53] *Comprehensive Program Report 2013* (Denpasar, Bali, Indonesia: Institute for Peace and Democracy, 2013).

[54] President Yudhoyono, interview with the author, Jakarta, 16 January 2014.

[55] Dr N. Hassan Wirajuda, "Indonesia's role in the Promotion of Democracy", Paper presented at The Brookings Institution, 28 April 2014, p. 9.

[56] Ibid., p. 10.

[57] Ketut Erawan, interview with the author, Dempasar, Bali, 6 January 2014.

[58] Wirajuda, op. cit., p. 10.

[59] Ketut Erawan, op. cit.

[60] Ibid.

[61] Wirajuda, op. cit., p. 11.

[62] Ketut Erawan, op. cit.

[63] Santo Darmosumarto, "Indonesia and the Asia-Pacific: Opportunities and Challenges for Middle Power Diplomacy", Policy Brief, The German Marshall Fund of the United States, July 2013, <http://www.gmfus.org/wp-content/blogs.dir/1/files_mf/1373398834Darmosumarto_Indonesia_Jul13.pdf>

64 Natalie Sambhi, "Indonesia's push for peacekeeping operations", 17 September 2013 <http://www.aspistrategist.org.au/indonesias-push-for-peacekeeping-operations/>

65 Yayan G.H. Mulyana, "Peacekeeping operations and Indonesian foreign policy", 3 January 2012 <http://www.thejakartapost.com/news/2012/01/03/peacekeeping-operations-and-indonesian-foreign-policy.html>

66 Rizal Sukma, "Indonesia's Security Outlook, Defense Policy and Regional Cooperation", p. 23 <http://www.nids.go.jp/english/publication/joint_research/series5/pdf/5-1.pdf>

Chapter 6

A NATION ON THE MOVE
Indonesian Voices

On 20 October 2014, Susilo Bambang Yudhoyono will have completed his second and final term as the President of Indonesia. The first popularly elected president of the country to complete two terms in office, he has presided over a country which has defied all the grim predictions after the downfall of the Suharto regime in 1998.

Recalling the dark days after Suharto's downfall, Fauzi Ichsan, an Indonesian economist, remembered (as quoted in the 23 January 2005 issue of the Bloomberg Business Week Magazine), "the betting was not whether Indonesia would fall apart – breaking into half a dozen island states – but how soon". Fifteen years later, in his keynote speech to the World Movement for Democracy, President Yudhoyono said:

> We proved the skeptics wrong. Indonesia's democracy has grown from strength to strength. We held three peaceful periodic national elections, in 1999, in 2004, and in 2009. We peacefully resolved the conflict in Aceh, with a democratic spirit, and pursued political and economic reforms in Papua. We made human rights protection a national priority. We pushed forward ambitious decentralization. Rather than regressing, Indonesia is progressing.[1]

The world outside has taken note and is in general agreement. Indonesia today is a respected member of the international community. It plays an important role not only in the Asia-Pacific region, but also in the world at large. Unfortunately, however, the Indonesian story receives far less attention than the BRICS (Brazil, Russia, India, China, and South Africa).

Yet in some respects the Indonesian story matters more than most of the other emerging powers. It matters because it tells the world three things which are not usually accepted by policymakers and analysts in Asia and elsewhere.

The first is that democracy, development and stability can go hand in hand and indeed create a virtuous cycle, and that democratization is conducive not only to development but also to national stability and regional order.

A second message from Indonesia can be described as follows: if you want to have status and legitimacy in international affairs you need to take the region with you. Fulfilling your global aspirations requires achieving a degree of regional legitimacy. In other words, to be a globally respectable actor, you cannot bully your neighbours but have to earn their trust and respect.

A third lesson from Indonesia is that a country can rise by exercising normative power and influence. Purely material capacity, including military strength, by itself is not the only way to attain status in international affairs. A country's normative positions, resources and roles are also the key.

While some of these lessons have been evident in the case of Western nations, especially the Scandinavian countries (which are nonetheless rich and some in cases militarily powerful) they are rarely found in the non-Western world, where being an emerging power is understood to need material capacity with normative resources and a role coming as a supplement. In the case of Indonesia, they have preceded material capacity. In this sense, Indonesia's path to emerging power status is an exceptional one.

But Indonesia faces many challenges that can potentially derail the country's recent achievements, including its democratic vitality, economic performance, domestic stability and international role. Corruption remains a major problem, although there has recently been growing vigilance and prosecution of corrupt officials. There is uncertainty over whether the next president will adopt an internationalist foreign policy outlook. There remain pockets of internal strife, in places such as West Papua, and the potential for outbreak of terrorism remains. Indonesia's limited bureaucratic capacity to conduct international affairs is another challenge. Externally, the rise of China, the growing rivalry among the major Asia-Pacific powers, China, Japan, US and India, may prove too much for Indonesia to handle.

What lies in store for Indonesia then? To continue its remarkable journey as Asia's emerging democratic power, Indonesia needs to guard against five major challenges. These challenges relate to its democracy, development, stability, external strategic environment and finally, foreign policy capacity and leadership. To get a sense of how these challenges may work out, let me provide some voices from within Indonesia.

Democracy

Seventy-eight year-old Sidarto Danusubroto is the oldest lawmaker in the Indonesian Parliament.[2] He is the Speaker of Majelis Permusyawaratan Rakyat (MPR- People's Consultative Assembly). He has lived through both the downfall and the revival of democracy in Indonesia. As Sukarno's aide during his final days of his house arrest by the new Suharto regime, he recalls the former president's sense of disillusionment and betrayal. A member of the opposition PDI-P party (Indonesian Democratic Party – Struggle), Danusubroto was elected three times (from 1999 to 2013) to the lower house of the Indonesian Parliament, the People's Representative Council, (Dewan Perwakilan Rakyat – DPR). He is close to both party supremo Megawati Sukarnoputri (who made him Honorary Party Chairman for 2009–14) and to Jakarta Governor and Presidential aspirant Joko Widodo (Jokowi).[3] He is also a former member of the House of Representatives Commission I on information, defence and foreign affairs.

I ask: "Is Indonesia's democracy working?" He replies, "Not so well." Asked to elaborate, he says, "Successful working of democracy requires a knowledgeable society and relatively high income levels. Indonesia's knowledge base and literacy levels are too low and the poverty level is too high." Another factor is money politics. "Every time I go to my constituency, I must bring lots of money," he says. The Speaker points to the "low quality" of candidates fielded by the political parties. There are "many beautiful people" who are "silent most of the time". These "beautiful silent people" refers to the celebrity legislators, including actors/actresses in the DPR. Most members cannot do "technical work, [such as] drafting of bills".[4] Former DPR member and chairman of Komisi I, Kemal Stamboel, left the parliament "disillusioned". Among the reasons was the low quality of parliamentary debates. The overall message: "The process of democracy in Indonesia has emerged but the substance of democracy is yet to be created."[5]

But Speaker Danusubroto is also adamant that the Suharto period was worse. Then the corrupt were "untouchable", the country's provincial governors were from the active army. The justice system was a military tribunal system. He also dismisses the yearning for Suharto in today's Indonesia (and there have been instances of Suharto's posters appearing in parts of the country) as a false one.

More importantly, Indonesians from all sectors of society have overwhelmingly chosen to take up the opportunity provided by democratization to participate in politics and use these democratic institutions to change Indonesia. Nearly without exception, these changes have redistributed power from the hands of a few (elites, TNI, the executive branch) to the hands of many. At the same time, Indonesia's political openness has been grounded in economic development and internal stability, which have provided Indonesian leaders with the political leeway to embark on reform programmes. A vast majority of Indonesians believes that democracy is the only suitable governance system for their country – it is "the only game in town."

But Indonesia's democratic progress should not be taken for granted. There is always the potential for some rollback on political and civic freedoms. There is a recent warning signal. In 1997, Indonesia was classified as a "Not Free" country in the Freedom House's *Freedom in the World* survey due to a lack of political rights (with a score of 7) and inadequate civil liberties (score of 5). As soon as Reformasi took place, Indonesia was upgraded to "Partly Free", a status it maintained as reformers worked on consolidating the democratization effort. The scores for its political rights and civil liberties continued to improve, and in 2006, Indonesia reached the milestone "Free" classification with a score of 2 for political rights and 3 for civil liberties. The trigger for this change was Indonesia's adoption of direct elections for provincial governors and district heads.[6] It was the only country in Southeast Asia to hold that label. After holding this classification for eight years, however, that status was downgraded back to "Partly Free" in 2014.[7] It continues to hold the "most free" political rights rating in Southeast Asia (a score of 2), for its free and fair elections held according to democratic principles. But its civil liberties score worsened (to 4). This downgrade was due to the Indonesian Parliament's approval of the 2013 Law on Mass Organizations.[8] The law requires NGOs to follow the Pancasila, support the unitary state of Indonesia, and receive government approval to operate. Most critically, in a throwback to the Suharto years, the law allows the government to suspend NGOs with little explanation.

Indonesia faces problems in other areas related to civil liberties as well. The aforementioned battle over the rights of Indonesia's religious minorities appears to favour religious conservatives who would seek to limit these rights. One big problem is the controversial blasphemy law, which protects Indonesia's six official religions from "defamation" by forbidding the expression of beliefs contrary to those espoused by these religions. The law remains on the books, having been upheld in 2010 by the Constitutional Court.

But no Indonesian I have talked to believes that the country is likely to undergo a complete reversal in democracy. Democracy remains too popular of an idea among Indonesian citizens. Pointing out that by the end of the first ten years after Suharto's rule ended, over three-quarters of Indonesians "believed in democratic governance", former Foreign Minister Hassan Wirajuda argues: "Indonesia's transition to democracy had reached a point of no return. Today democracy is entrenched as a national value."[9]

Assessing Indonesia's democratic future, Larry Diamond notes, "…democracy in Indonesia will not stand or fall on how well it is doing relative to other democracies in the world. It will stand or fall in terms of how well it is doing in itself."[10] He cited governance issues as potential trouble spots, especially corruption and governance issues.[11] A free and democratic nation allows its people to choose its future, but those elected to guide the nation forward must be committed to and capable of safeguarding the democratic polity. But neither corruption nor poor governance are new problems in Indonesia. Certainly on both counts, Indonesia needs to improve. A less-corrupt Indonesia will be better able to allocate government resources to support the needs of its growing population, will attract more foreign investment in its preferred industries, and will secure the trust of its people. But corruption probably will not worsen unless the KPK (Komisi Pemberantasan Korupsi, or Corruption Eradication Commission) is defanged. In order to do so, however, the government would have to circumvent the Constitution as well as the will of the people who strongly support the anti-corruption commission. The KPK is currently under parliamentary pressure to curtail its investigate powers again, but it has weathered such storms before.

But unless the "quality of democracy" increases, politicians may use popular frustration over the slow pace or back-and-forth nature of the reform process to roll back democratic rights. Even then, an outright reversal of democratic gains is highly unlikely. One reason for this, says Rizal Sukma, is the pluralistic nature of the Indonesian polity, and the nature of the party system which ensures that no political party achieves a dominant position in the election. The parties offset each other. Moreover, the Islamic parties have joined the game, realizing that democracy is key to the survival of political Islam.[12] Kemal Stamboel, the former parliamentarian, "strongly believes" that reversal of democracy won't happen in Indonesia because of a system of checks and balances. He points to legislative vigilance. The "parliament can push a president back if he falls into backsliding". The DPR wields the threat of impeachment. What if the leader of a party with a large majority did a legislative coup? In that case, he argues, the constitutional court can nullify legislation to create authoritarianism. And "student groups will rise up".[13]

What about a military takeover? This is also seen as highly unlikely. During a visit to Makassar in March 2014, South Sulawesi, I had an extensive discussion with Major General Bachtiar (like many Indonesians, he goes by a single name) and his staff about, among other issues, the political role of the military and the relationship between the military and society. Major General Bachtiar is the commander of Kodam VII/Wirabuana, which oversees all provinces on the Sulawesi island. A product of the Suharto era, as the graduate of the 1984 batch of the National Military Academy in Magelang, he insists that "democracy in Indonesia is number one in the world", providing a variety of freedoms to Indonesians.[14] He believes that Indonesia's democratic transition is an "extraordinary" achievement and that the civilian control of the military is irreversible. So is the formal and legalized abolition of the military's business interests. These business interests are not necessary, because of a higher defence budget.

To be sure, the scope of the military's functions is an expansive one. Major General Bachtiar counts the missions of the military to include: countering separatism, armed rebellions, terrorism, ensuring the security of citizens, international peacekeeping, protection of the President, Vice-President and their families, providing assistance to local governments and police, protection of foreign dignitaries, responding to natural disasters, conducting search and rescue missions, and fighting against militancy, piracy, and smuggling.[15] But this is a far cry from the *dwifungsi* (or dual function), the old doctrine that legitimized the military's role in politics. While the military can assist the police in maintaining domestic law and order, or provide direct assistance to the people in time of crisis, he does not see here a risk of interference in politics. Instead such a role in civilian protection is necessary lest the military be accused of negligence.

Speaker Danusubroto would agree. A relapse of military rule in Indonesia, is "not going to be easy. The military is not so solid (united) now, things are different [from the Suharto period]." Moreover, "They [the military] have learnt about human rights, democracy. Return to power not easy."[16] His main concern, however, is that the military is not subject to anti-corruption investigations by the KPK. This needs to be rectified. Riefiqi Muna, a researcher at the Indonesian Institute of Sciences (LIPI),[17] points to another reason why return to military rule would be unlikely. The process of security sector reform in Indonesia, he notes, "was self-directed, not imposed by politicians". This is a unique feature of Indonesia's security sector reform, and it happened because of the Reformasi movement, or pressure from people. It also happened because the military realized that Suharto was no longer in control. There was an internalization of democratic norms and ideals among senior military officers including General (later President) Yudhoyono.

What about Thailand, which many analysts in the 1990s had thought would never return to military coups? Yet it did so. But the Indonesian situation is different in an important respect: it does not have the monarchy whose protection has become the focal point of a class divide in Thailand. But things could change, especially if democracy does not deliver the economic goods to the people.

Development

Mahendra Siregar, Chairman, Indonesia Investment Coordinating Board (BKPM), insists that the "middle-income trap" is not an option for Indonesia. He points out that Indonesia will be facing a demographic bonus for the next 15–18 years.[18] This is both a challenge and an opportunity. If these young Indonesians are able to make a substantially positive contribution to Indonesia's economy, Indonesia could see record rates of growth in the decades to come. But they will not reach their potential unless the government ensures that they can all enjoy an improved educational system that prepares them to take on skilled jobs. At the same time, the Indonesian economy will have to grow fast enough to guarantee that these young workers are both employed and supported by a widened government-funded social safety net.

Economic development may well be the area where Indonesia is most vulnerable. Some foreign analysts suggest that to preserve its progress on this front, Indonesian policymakers need to avert protectionist policies which could slow economic growth and hinder foreign investment. Indonesia's middle class is also a consuming, urbanizing class, and investing in infrastructure and reducing inequality are crucial to ensure that growth is able to keep pace with the demand for jobs.

Indonesian policymakers are well-aware that infrastructure needs to be improved, and they have started to back up their verbal statements with financial resources. The ratio of infrastructure spending to the overall budget was 2.5 per cent five years ago. It is now 3 per cent, with an additional 2 per cent from private or public/private spending, to make an improved ratio of 5 per cent.[19] Foreign direct investment could significantly boost infrastructure investment, but in this regard Indonesia needs to get out of its own way and stop sending mixed signals to foreign investors by passing confusing regulations that are heavy with red-tape.

Indonesia's main challenge at this juncture is navigating the transition from a middle-income developing country to an industrialized, advanced economy, and avoiding the notorious "middle-income trap" that has trapped its neighbour Malaysia. This is a long-term challenge and a very difficult one. With 20 per cent of Indonesians now in middle-class status, the government will need to respond to the desires of this new consumer class for a better life. At the same time, the government must take care that Indonesia's poor are not left behind by this transition. Maintaining inefficient fuel subsidies and discouraging foreign investment are not necessarily the way to protect Indonesia's poor, however. Economic reform may be politically painful in the short-term, but its pay-offs could be long-lasting and necessary.

Another challenge to Indonesia's economic prospects comes from economic nationalism., especially when it comes to control over natural resources. The government's restriction on certain type of mining activities, extremely unpopular with investors, is partly the result of such resource nationalism. Danusubroto has lent voice to such sentiments: "Foreign powers dominate the economy and our development. Idealism as shown by Sukarno and other leaders are now tainted by interest groups and money. We must go back to the independence of the nation as taught by Bung Karno."[20] Some Indonesians feel that the country has gone too far in embracing the market. With 50 million people still poor in

Indonesia, and inequality widening, there is a demand for more poor-friendly policies and more affirmative action.[21]

Stability

Even democratic countries like India face serious internal security challenges, including separatism and insurgency (as has been the case in India in recent years with the Maoist rebellion affecting more than a dozen states). President Yudhoyono is cautious when he speaks of Indonesia's domestic stability. "Indonesia is more stable than Thailand", but the stability is "not to be taken for granted".[22] But the outlook is far more positive today than it was a decade ago. Rizal Sukma argues that in Indonesia, the fear of "balkanisation" has given way to confidence for three reasons: (1) peaceful, democratic elections, (2) ability to deal with internal conflicts, such as in Aceh, Poso, and the Molukus, where communal violence was brought to an end, and (3) success in getting the military to play by the book. In his view, Indonesia's "bond of nationhood – the feeling of Indonesianness – is much stronger" than outsiders believe.[23] This author agrees.

As long as decentralization and autonomy initiatives are maintained, and the central government continues to support economic development in previously-neglected provinces, Indonesia's internal conflicts are most likely to remain under control. This does not mean that Indonesia should reduce its vigilance. The fact that the 2014 parliamentary elections were without a hitch is promising. (Three people were killed in drive-by shootings shortly before the elections in Aceh – the incident raised some alarm bells as they appeared to be politically-motivated.)[24] In addition, the government needs to stabilize through peaceful means the last two provinces to suffer from regular conflict, Papua and West Papua.

It is unlikely at this point that either province will launch a successful separatist movement, but there are lingering worries about human rights violations inflicted by the Indonesian authorities. It is in Indonesia's interest to remedy the situation as soon as possible, not only because the residents of Papua and West Papua should be able to enjoy the same daily stability and security as all other Indonesian citizens, but also because this conflict challenges Indonesia's otherwise positive international image. Vanuatu, for instance, suggested to the UN Human Rights Council on 4 March 2014, that it adopt a mandate on the human rights situation in West Papua.[25] Under President Yudhoyono, Indonesia has made much progress repairing its international reputation and assuring the global community that it respects human rights. It would be a shame for Southeast Asia's pioneering advocate for R2P to require international pressure to address an internal conflict.

External Environment

Indonesia's Foreign Minister Marty Natalegawa is not a person given to showing signs of anxiety and stress in public. Yet he admits that developments in the region are making him "less comfortable in his sleep".[26] Indonesia's external environment is becoming more complex and challenging. The early post-Cold War sense of optimism about regional order has dissipated and China's recent assertiveness in the region has sparked anxieties in Asian capitals, including Jakarta. As noted, Indonesia now accepts that China's nine-dash line in the South China Sea overlaps with waters off Indonesia's Natuna island chain, thereby setting the stage for a more confrontational relationship with China. While Indonesia continues to stress its role as a moderator and facilitator in the South China Sea conflict, a further deterioration of the Natuna situation will affect this role negatively.

Another challenge to Indonesian's position as a regional mediator comes from the US policy of rebalancing or "pivot" in the Indo-Pacific. The US has been positive and far-sighted in developing ties with democratic Indonesia. Moreover, the Obama Administration has been careful in not forcing its agenda on ASEAN and ASEAN-led regional forums where Indonesia plays a central role. Washington continues to adhere to the principle of ASEAN centrality. But if relations between the US and China deteriorate further, it will test that principle. Hence much depends on Jakarta's ability to secure a code of conduct on the South China Sea, which is by no means assured. If regional order collapse it will call into question the "million friends and zero enemies" policy, which some of its critics already regard as "only dreaming".[27]

Foreign Policy Capacity and Leadership

Natalegawa also admits to another challenge to Indonesia's foreign policy role, when he says disarmingly, "I fear we are firing on all cylinders." With democratization, and the consequent advent of multiple domestic stakeholders, ownership and participation in foreign policy making, the instant social media, and a 24/7 news cycle, he has "no time to think". He has to get used to "making policy on the run". The Indonesian Foreign Ministry needs more than diplomats, needs broader expertise on complex transnational issues which increasingly confront Indonesia and the region.[28]

Finally, Indonesia's role as an emerging power is affected by the issue of leadership. This has several aspects. One is the style of leadership. Western nations, not familiar with Indonesia's low-key and impartial approach, are sometimes exasperated with Indonesia's low-key approach, its refusal to speak loud and clear, and its tendency to take a balanced position on some especially contentious issues like humanitarian intervention. One senior Western diplomat who did not want to be identified told me that "to play a global leadership role, you sometimes need to take sides". This was with reference to Indonesia's overly cautious approach to the intervention in Libya. In this view, Indonesia's neutral and – a "million friends and no enemies" – approach can sometimes be a handicap in global governance.

Another issue of leadership is presidential leadership. There are concerns within and outside Indonesia about how leadership change will also affect Indonesia's foreign policy and role. It can only be expected that some presidents of Indonesia would be more active in foreign policy than others. This may be due not only to domestic preoccupations and constraints, as happened immediately after the fall of Suharto, but also to personal preference and interest. But President Yudhoyono's very active engagement in foreign policy makes the issue more moot. Would a future Indonesian President be as interested and involved in foreign policy, in pushing Indonesia's profile around the world?[29] While some Indonesians worry about this, others such as Hassan Wirajuda, dismiss such concerns. Much depends on the team the President brings with him/her, including the Foreign Minister and the Ministry to run the conduct of foreign policy.[30] Another concern is whether a President with a controversial past might gain the office and create problems between Indonesia and the West.[31]

Analysing the prospects for a major shift in Indonesia's foreign policy after Yudhoyono, Donald K. Emmerson notes, "But even if an inward shift in official attention does occur, it will not undo the record of interest in foreign affairs already compiled by Yudhoyono."[32] Yet, it remains to be seen whether his successor would pursue the kind of "tactful, eclectic and multilateralist foreign policy" (in Emmerson's words) that Yudhoyono has pursued.

Indonesia's ability to avoid collapse and rebuild itself is one of the most impressive stories of the late 20th and early 21st century. Its journey since the fall of Suharto is all the more inspiring at a time when the world has seen many failing nations, recurring economic crises, and growing radicalism and terrorism. In foreign policy, the course charted by Indonesia seems well set and would continue to guide Indonesian foreign policy and regional and global role. Observing Indonesia at different levels does create the sense that whereas there was too little expectation about Indonesia in 1998–99, now there is too much. No one can dismiss the possibility that Indonesia might not be able to live up to such expectations. But it also seems reasonable to believe that Indonesia's leadership is likely to continue to receive international recognition and support as long as its democracy continues to progress alongside development and stability. Ultimately, it is these domestic factors which will decide Indonesia's regional and global role as an emerging power.

While this book does not discuss the implications of the outcome of the 9 July 2014 presidential election, the five factors outlined in the conclusion – democracy, development, stability, external strategic environment, and foreign policy capacity and leadership, are extremely relevant in assessing Indonesia's future progress and role as an emerging power under the new president. Nevertheless, thinking ahead, the outcome of the 2014 presidential election could present a challenge to Indonesia's international role.

The closely contested polls and the low margin of victory of the winner not only create an air of political uncertainty, but could also affect the legitimacy and authority of the presidency in crafting and directing foreign policy, because of distractions caused by the need to devote more attention and political capital to managing domestic competition and uncertainty.

In a political system in which the presidential authority is subject to serious legislative checks and balances, this could weaken the president's hand in foreign policy. Furthermore, the election revealed a divide between the forces of economic nationalism and that of economic internationalism, and between those who prefer "strong" government despite the risk of authoritarianism, and those who want to keep pushing Indonesia on the path to further political liberalization. While hardly unusual in a non-Western democracy, these divides are especially challenging to Indonesia's still young democracy and given its political diversity.

The election also illustrated disagreements between a position (adopted by Joko Widodo) that calls for greater use of diplomacy and negotiations to resolve regional and international problems, and that (indicated by Prabowo Subianto) which would prefer a power-based approach, stressing the build-up of military strength. While this divide can be overstated, ultimately Indonesia will need both hard power and diplomacy to become a significant emerging power in the Asia-Pacific and the world. A retreat from democracy could cause a significant setback to its international reputation and aspirations.

In assessing the emergence of Indonesia from the dark period following Suharto's downfall, what is also strikingly clear is that some of the most perceptive assessments of the country's achievements and limitations come from Indonesians themselves. Instead of hubris, I note a quiet confidence, a guarded sense of optimism. But there was also an acute awareness of Indonesia's weaknesses in making continuing progress and criticisms of the country's politics, leaders and developmental objectives. In a country where criticisms and self-doubt were rarely permitted during the long years of Suharto's rule, this in itself is a remarkable sign of progress. My conversations tell me that Indonesia is no longer a *nation in waiting*, but is a *nation on the move*.

Notes

[1] Susilo Bambang Yudhoyono, Keynote Speech for the World Movement for Democracy, 12 April 2010. <http://www.wmd.org/assemblies/sixth-assembly/remarks/keynote-speech-dr-susilo-bambang-yudhoyono>

[2] Sidarto Danusubroto, interview with the author, Jakarta, 18 March 2014.

[3] The evening before I met him, he had dinner with Jokowi, who himself had just been nominated by Megawati as the official PDI-P candidate for the Indonesian presidency.

[4] Sidarto Danusubroto, interview with the author, Jakarta, 18 March 2014.

[5] Kemal Stamboel, interview with the author, Jakarta, 12 March 2014.

[6] Alexander R. Arifianto, "Is Indonesia Experiencing a 'Democratic Rollback'?" ISEAS Perspective, 27 February 2014, p. 2. <http://www.iseas.edu.sg/documents/publication/ISEAS_Perspective_2014_11-Is_Indonesia_Experiencing_a_Democractic_Rollback.pdf>

7   <http://www.freedomhouse.org/country/indonesia#.U11TUvldWp0>

8   Arifianto, p. 7.

9   Dr N. Hassan Wirajuda, "Indonesia's role in the Promotion of Democracy", Paper presented at The Brookings Institution, 28 April 2014, p. 4.

10 Larry Diamond, "How is Indonesia's democracy doing?" *East Asia Forum*, 26 October 2009 <http://www.eastasiaforum.org/2009/10/26/how-is-indonesias-democracy-doing/>

11 Ibid.

12 Rizal Sukma, interview with the author, 10 March 2014.

13 Kemal Stamboel, interview with the author, Jakarta, 12 March 2014.

14 Major General Bachtiar, conversation with the author, Makassar, South Sulawesi, 17 March 2014. Gen Bachitar was accompanied by a dozen of his senior staff.

15 Ibid.

16 Sidarto Danusubroto, interview with the author, Jakarta, 18 March 2014.

17 Riefiqi Muna, interview with the author, Jakarta, 19 January 2014.

18 Mahendra Siregar, interview with the author, 10 March 2014.

19 Ibid.

20 Asvi Warman Adam, "Sidarto Danusubroto: From Sukarno aide to MPR Speaker", *Jakarta Post*, 18 July 2013 <http://www.thejakartapost.com/news/2013/07/18/sidarto-danusubroto-from-sukarno-aide-mpr-speaker.html>

21 Kemal Stamboel, interview with the author, Jakarta, 12 March 2014.

22 President Yudhoyono, interview with the author, Jakarta, 16 January 2014.

23 Rizal Sukma, interview with the author, Jakarta, 10 March 2014.

24 Hotli Simanjuntak, "Three people slain in drive-by shooting in Aceh." *Jakarta Post*, 2 April 2014 <http://www.thejakartapost.com/news/2014/04/02/three-people-slain-drive-shooting-aceh.html>

25 Budi Hernawan, "Is a UN resolution on Papua impossible?" *Jakarta Post, 21* March 2014 <http://www.thejakartapost.com/news/2014/03/21/is-a-un-resolution-papua-impossible.html>

26 Marty Natalegawa, interview with the author, Jakarta, 20 January 2014.

27 Sidarto Danusubroto, interview with the author, Jakarta, 18 March 2014.

28 Marty Natalegawa, interview with the author, Jakarta, 20 January 2014.

29 This issue was raised during the 2014 elections with reference to Jokowi as someone with little foreign policy experience who some felt would be more engaged in domestic reform and management. But Danusubroto, who is personally close to Jokowi, insists that although he has no foreign policy experience, "his answers to foreign policy questions are smart". He discusses the foreign policy of Sukarno, but will not bring back Sukarno's foreign policy. But

there will be "more balance between foreign and domestic affairs" under Jokowi. Sidarto Danusubroto, interview with the author, Jakarta, 18 March 2014.

30   Hassan Wirajuda, op. cit.

31   During the 2014 elections, such a concern was raised about Lt General Probowo, the Presidential candidate of the GERINDRA (Great Indonesia Movement Party). Given his association with the Suharto regime (he was married to one of Suharto's daughters) and his role in human rights abuses by the Indonesian Armed Forces, his election could undermine Indonesia's "image" in the international arena as a democratic power.

32   Donald K. Emmerson, "Is Indonesia Rising: It Depends", in Anthony J. S. Reid, ed., *Indonesia Rising: The Repositioning of Asia's Third Giant* (Singapore: Institute of Southeast Asian Studies, 2012).

ABOUT THE AUTHOR

AMITAV ACHARYA is the UNESCO Chair in Transnational Challenges and Governance, Chair of the ASEAN Studies Center, and Professor of International Relations at the School of International Service, American University, Washington, D.C.

He has held professorial appointments at York University, Toronto; University of Bristol, UK; and Nanyang Technological University, Singapore. He was Fellow of the Asia Center and John F. Kennedy School of Government, Harvard University, US; Nelson Mandela Visiting Professor in International Relations at Rhodes University, South Africa; and was elected to the Christensen Fellowship at St Catherine's College, Oxford.

His books on Southeast Asia include *The Making of Southeast Asia: International Relations of a Region* (Cornell 2013; a significantly revised and updated version of *The Quest for Identity: International Relations of Southeast Asia* published by Oxford in 2000); *Constructing a Security Community in Southeast Asia* (Routledge 2001, 2009, 2014); and *Whose Ideas Matter? Agency and Power in Asian Regionalism* (Cornell 2009).

His books on global affairs include *The End of American World Order* (Polity 2014); and *Rethinking Power, Institutions and Ideas in World Politics* (Routledge 2013).

His articles have appeared in dozens of journals including *International Organization, International Security, International Studies Quarterly, Journal of Asian Studies, Journal of Peace Research, Pacific Review, Pacific Affairs* and *World Politics*.

He has appeared frequently in international media, including CNN International, BBC TV, BBC World Service Radio, Al-Jazeera TV, CNBC, CTV (Canada), CBC (Canada), and Radio Australia and written op-eds for *Financial Times, foreignaffairs.com, International Herald Tribune, Huffington Post, Times of*

India, Indian Express, The Hindu, Straits Times, Australian Financial Review, Far Eastern Economic Review, Japan Times, Jakarta Post, South China Morning Post, and YaleGlobal Online.

He is the President of the International Studies Association (ISA) for 2014–15 (full bio at www.amitavacharya.com)Twitter: @AmitavAcharya